# *No*
# *No Aversions*

*THE AUTOBIOGRAPHY OF A MASTER*

*by Lester Levenson*

## An American Master's Own Story to Spiritual Enlightenment

Publisher:

Lawrence Crane Enterprises, Inc.
15101 Rayneta Drive
Sherman Oaks, CA 91403
Phone: 888-333-7703 or 818-385-0611
Fax: 818-385-0563
Email: ReleaseLA@aol.com
Web site: www.releasetechnique.com

Printed in the United States of America

Library of Congress number TX5-021-629

For the first time, a living American Master tells the story of his life and details step by step in simple, everyday English how he achieved the extraordinary powers of omniscience, omnipresence, and omnipotence.

This twentieth century Master came into his immortality not by the shores of the Ganges, nor on the heights of the Himalayas, but in the bustling heart of New York City.

In the past, anyone who has sought information and understanding of ultimate happiness and peace has had to turn to the exotic teachings of the East.

Lester Levenson—born in New Jersey, a former physicist and businessman—points the way to freedom that Westerners can readily understand and follow.

Larry Crane

Lawrence Crane

Author and teacher of Lester's "Release Technique"

# *No Attachments No Aversions*

## *CONTENTS*

# *Introduction*

When I think this book is going to be about me, I get cringing feelings. It's not easy for me to be an ego and yet I must talk as an ego in order to communicate.

Once you see your real inner Self, it's very difficult to identify as a separate individual—an ego.

But I can go through with the telling of this story.

I fell into something that everyone is looking for. I had no idea it was there. All of my desires were fulfilled; all my miseries dropped away; all my sicknesses disappeared.

I came into an exalted state of happiness, so tremendous, it is difficult to describe.

This joy is what everyone in the world is seeking.

This is what very few people are finding.

But the way this fell upon me can be given to others, so that it can fall upon them also.

I'm talking about something that hardly anyone has yet experienced. How can I describe it?

No limits on anything in any direction whatsoever. The ability to do anything for the mere thought of it. Yet it is more than that.

Imagine the highest joy you can have, multiply it by a hundred, and tell me what it is.

You will only feel it to the degree that you're capable of feeling it, experiencing it. It can't be gotten intellectually through the mind.

Imagine being madly in love with your mate and embracing your mate, with your mind on nothing else but the joy of the embrace. Now double that for two people, quadruple it for four people, and then make it four billion times greater by including the four billion people on earth.

That's the feeling.

Lester Levenson

# B.C.

## Life Before Consciousness

## *Love is Trust*

I was an average guy seeking happiness in money and women, battling my way through life like everyone else. Never finding it, I continued banging my head so hard on the brick wall of the world that I almost smashed my brains out. I had ulcers, migraine, jaundice, kidney stones and finally a coronary attack which put me near death.

That extremity drove me into the right direction, to the knowledge of what life is all about.

This knowledge gave me contentment, actually a peace which cannot be disturbed. People can yell at me, scream, do anything, and the peace in the background never changes.

It's there all the time.

I was a rebel against society and I banged my head on its brick wall until I discovered the way out.

Now that I have discovered it, others don't have to bang their head so hard to find it. It's available for anyone who wants it.

Anyone who really wants the knowledge and freedom gets it. All you need is you—and the desire for it. You are the book. You are the real book. An intense desire for it opens up the real you to you.

That's what happens. But we're so plagued with blindness today that we need a teacher, one who knows and can keep pointing out the way.

Within you is unlimited power, knowledge and intelligence. You just open yourself up to that which you subconsciously already know, have always known and always will know.

From the beginning, I was bewildered. I couldn't understand the world. I rebelled against it, yet I wanted to do right, be right with the world. From post-college days on until 1952, I just kept trying to do what I thought was the correct thing.

I had a degree in physics and I wanted to be the world's greatest physicist. I was graduated from college in 1931. No jobs for physicists then, so I shifted into engineering. I worked as an aeronautical, civil, mechanical, electrical, marine and construction engineer.

I'd get a job and wouldn't last a year because it just didn't feel right. So I'd go into another type of engineering and yet another. I tried going into business for myself. I've been in many businesses, again for short periods of time. I'd get them successful, lose interest, then lose them.

I just kept changing and changing, never understanding why until 1952. Then I realized what I was looking for was not in a job or business. No job, no business, even when I was into it and successful, could give it to me.

During my whole life, I was unconsciously seeking what I discovered in 1952.

## *MYSELF.*

I was born in Elizabeth, New Jersey, July 19, 1909.

My earliest recollection was of water. I always loved water.

When I was four, I used to walk two long blocks and two short blocks to a large docking and recreation wharf in Elizabethport.

I'd climb up on a wall at the edge of the dock—it was about two feet high and about three feet wide—and I'd just lie down on it with my head over the edge watching the water flow by for hours at a time, for so many hours that my mother went looking for me. When she found me, she almost collapsed seeing me, a tot, hanging over the edge of the dock and gently took me by the hand and with a smile said, "Come on home." She never scolded me. She just told me I shouldn't do that because I might fall in.

But I never fell in. I didn't believe it.

Liking the water so much I'd wander back to the dock.

Even as a child I wasn't believing what others told me. My mother warned me that green bananas made people sick. I used to love bananas. I had eaten green bananas and had not gotten sick. So to prove a point, one day I ate a dozen green bananas and said, "Look, Ma! I feel fine!'"

She just laughed.

My mother used to get a delight out of me. Here I was, so little and acting like a grown-up, teaching her by proving things to her.

> ***"We are unlimited beings— limited only by the concepts of limitation we hold in our minds."***

My mother was an unusually loving person. Never in her whole lifetime did she ever scold me. Never.

She was so good, whatever she asked, you had to do it for her. Not only I, but my three sisters did the same thing. We could never refuse her because she herself went way out of her way to help us all the time. She never said "No" to us. Wouldn't even "No" us on anything.

When she died, mobs and mobs of people came to the funeral and we never expected it. She loved every person she met. What a winning personality! All of my friends, everyone, loved her.

She was the real guiding light in the family.

She was so very giving. I'd come home, get undressed and throw my shoes and clothes all over the place. She'd follow after me and pick up, never with a harsh word.

My father was the opposite. "Now you do it or else…!" I'd defy him and then run to get behind my mother for protection.

When I became a teenager and was dating girls, she gently said, "Just be careful, Lester, Just be careful."

I said, "Don't worry, Mom. I know what I'm doing." I thought I was a man.

I was a bewildered, quiet, small child, always down at the end of the line in school because of my short height. My predominate characteristic was shyness.

It's a horrible thing being shy. In the first grade when I was supposed to recite a Christmas poem, my mother was so delighted, she diligently helped me learn it. I was trying not to, but I did learn it only to make her happy. Then I got sick the day of the Christmas party. I really played sick.

I did the same thing throughout high school and college. I never got up in front of the class. I was always out sick on days of oral compository when I would have had to speak to the class. I just couldn't. Even when a teacher called my name, I'd blush and blush, and feel incapacitated.

When I'd blush, people would say, "Look, he's blushing!" I would turn redder and redder and I just would want to die.

Even after college, if I'd see a girl I liked coming down the street, I'd walk around the block to avoid passing her, even if I were on the other side of the street. I used to die when approaching a girl I liked.

Yet I was able to force it, eventually, slowly, and the shyness would go away with that particular girl.

I was extremely withdrawn and introspective as a child, wondering what this life was all about. It never added up. I never felt as though I belonged to my family, to society. I could never understand the why of life itself. It never made any sense to me. I felt like a stranger in this world. That feeling I could never get away from. Until I got my realizations I never felt as though I belonged or fitted here.

Maybe it was a sense of this isn't the place to be in?

But I tried to fit in. I tried to do what was right. I tried to be as I was expected to be. Tried to be like everyone else was.

But I was always bewildered. Always wanted to know the why's and just had no answers to them.

My father, was a tall, very good-looking, egotistical fellow, nattily dressed all the time. He was not the intellectual type; he was interested in the usual goals of the world. My mother, on the other hand, was always interested in culture. When I was a kid, she'd take me to shows and museums in New York City. But dad stayed home.

She took me to Broadway shows, musicals, Barnum and Bailey Circuses. I guess it was her way of introducing me to culture and fun.

My parents wanted me to be a doctor or lawyer. My father used to brag all the time about me, except if I were present. Then he'd switch to the opposite. It was silly.

My father was very emotional; he would hug and kiss me in public, even when I was in my twenties. I thought it unmasculine and used to hate it. He was very warm and emotional that way.

My parents were not really religious, but my grandfathers on both sides were holy people, Rabbis. I've seen pictures of my great-grandfathers, very aristocratic and distinguished looking rabbis.

My grandfather left Russia to avoid having his sons pulled into the army. He bought a passport with the name Levenson on it. That's how I got my name. I was originally Prehonnica.

I have three sisters: Florence, a year and a half older than I, Doris, five years younger, and Naomi, ten years younger.

My father favored Florence. She would tease me and start a fight and I would always get blamed for it. I couldn't do anything about it.

But with my younger sisters I always got along beautifully. When my father passed on, I really became their father and took care of the family.

My kid sister has been like a baby to me always. Now she's a grandmother, but to me she's still a baby. I can understand now why eighty-year-old parents treat their sixty-year-old children like kids.

Our family was always close. My sisters and I used to meet after dates, around the refrigerator in the kitchen, one, two, three in the morning and talk for hours.

So it was a friendly group.

My father was a business man. He was in the grocery business. He had about half a dozen workers, and this was before the days of the A & P and chain stores.

We always lived a little better than most of the people around us. My father was never rich, though. In fact, during my adult life, he was usually in debt. The A & P put him out of the grocery business.

Then in the '20s my father went into real estate, pyramiding, owning lots of land everywhere. But in 1929, he did beautifully, and had a car—that was a big thing in those days.

Then in 1930 he opened up a luncheonette. Actually it was a stationery store, but I introduced sandwiches and coffee and it became more successful as a luncheonette.

The luncheonette was the center of the family until the sudden passing away of my mother because of pneumonia. My father never got over it. He became ill and for a year and a half gradually withered away from pining for our lost mother.

When my father passed on, my uncle wanted me to say the very sacred and holy prayer that you say for the dead. I looked him right in the eye and said, "Will that bring him back? If it does, I'll say it."

He just turned away.

I didn't say the prayer because I didn't think it would.

When my father passed on, I sort of became the father of the family. My youngest sister, Naomi, was in high school. Doris was already out of it, and Florence had begun teaching. She was really on her own.

And so, I took over as the head of the household and ran the luncheonette. When I took it over, it had a ten thousand dollar indebtness because of my father's illness.

And because it wasn't doing well, I held onto my job as an air conditioning engineer. I really worked around the clock keeping that place going.

My father left us with heavy debts. Wanting to uphold the honor of the family, I was determined to pay off all of the debts. So, I did a few little things to the store and it started making money. Within a year's time, I had the debts taken care of.

After my mother died, I missed her so much myself I couldn't sleep one night's sleep the first year. At the time, I thought grieving was the right thing to do. Now I know it was nothing but selfishness. I wanted the comfort of her being around me, to give me the love she used to give me. I missed the affection she had been giving me.

At that time I believed there was no life after death. Nothing was real except that which you could feel, sense, touch and prove right in front of your eyes. My beloved mother had become dust.

### *LOVE IS LOVING THE OTHER ONE BECAUSE THE OTHER ONE IS THE WAY THE OTHER ONE IS*

When I was a child the streets in Elizabeth were mostly unpaved dirt streets. Only the main street was paved with cobblestones. Horses and wagons were the way of transportation. Electricity wasn't in yet. We had gas lights, although all my neighborhood friends had homes with kerosene lamps.

My father took us out riding Sundays by hitching the horse to the surrey. People worked twelve hours a day, six days a week then. But they were friendlier. Come Sunday, we had picnics or would visit.

There was very little entertainment so people would get together for fun. It seemed a nicer way of life than today.

There was no radio, television or movies. I first remember movies around 1918. It cost 5 cents to see Pearl White, Tom Mix and all those serials.

I built a radio way back about 1920 when radio was in its infancy. I was in high school. Got an oatmeal box and wound some wire on it, put on a slide tuner, added a crystal and a pair of earphones, and to my surprise, it worked. The first song I heard was "Tomorrow, tomorrow, how happy I will be." It was such a thrill that I never forgot it.

I always had a tendency to like science and mechanics. I was always playing around up in the attic where I had an electronic lab, always experimenting with little gadgets.

As a child I'd take everything apart in the house. I'd take the clocks apart and usually get them working again with a few extra parts left over.

I was probably nine, ten years old when I took apart the player piano. Just got it together in time before my father got home.

I remember once taking the steel spring out of the victrola, and boy, what a job that was getting it back! It took me days, but they didn't use the thing, so I got away with it. With extreme, unusual forcing, I finally got that heavy steel spring back into its place and the victrola working again.

My parents knew my tendency and I was always being warned: Don't touch!

The first clock didn't work when I put it back together.

I remember being caught at something else.

I was nine years old. I was told I could have anything I wanted in the store. That led me into taking cigarettes.

It was the kids in the gang who encouraged me. I used to take a pack of cigarettes—Luckys—they still have them. Then we shifted to Camels.

We'd gather at night up in the hayloft, my father's hayloft for the horses, and would we be big-shots, smoking away. We even tried cigars one Saturday, and after the smoke we went swinging on the swing below the hayloft. The awful sickness and nausea that resulted finished any more interest in cigars.

I was so sick that my mother couldn't help noticing, although I was trying to hide it. I fought her calling in a doctor for fear he would know I was smoking cigars.

I once gave a cigarette to Doris. Doris was only four years old. She asked for it and I said, "Sure," and I gave it to her.

This was in the kitchen. I didn't know my father was around.

She took a big puff, breathed it in, and coughed and coughed and coughed. And just as she started to cough, in walked my father! Oh! Did I get it! Did he yell!

I scrammed. I left the house because I felt that this was going to be catastrophic.

In those days no good women smoked. It was really considered an evil thing to do. And you certainly did not give a girl four years old a cigarette.

In my elementary school days, parents were so busy making a living that we were on our own. When we came home from school, the first thing we'd do would be to get out on the street and meet the gang. With a broomstick as a bat, and a piece of it cut off as a caddy, we'd play ball. We'd also use tin cans to play duck-on-the-rock and other games devised by our ingenuity. There was really a good camaraderie amongst kids in those days.

We were fortunate in not being smothered by parental over-attention. We better learned how to take care of ourselves, an advantage we had over kids today.

I remember getting a bicycle for myself.

At the age of ten I prayed to God every night for a bicycle for half a year. But the bicycle didn't come. I wanted it so badly. I went into much thought. I realized I could get a job delivering newspapers and maybe buy one myself. I did get the job. At 50 cents a week the money didn't accumulate very fast, but it got me my first bicycle—a five-dollar, beat-up, second-hand one.

My mother, a great pacifist, taught me early that it's always better to run away from a fight than it is to fight. It was an awful thing to teach me, because in those days the kids were cruel and would gang up on me because I was a Jew and I was small.

One day I was on the ground with five of them punching away at me. I couldn't take it any more and lost my temper. I began furiously punching back. They started to run, and I was chasing all five of them!

I stopped suddenly and took a look. I said, "Oh my God! I used to die of fear of them and here they are, five of them running away from me!" I resolved, "Never again will I show any fear." I was nine years old and in the third grade at the time. That lesson never left me.

We moved around quite a lot during my school days. As soon as I'd enroll in a new school I knew from experience that the school bully was going to challenge me because I was a little Jew-boy. So I would quickly challenge the bully and scare him to the point where we wouldn't have to fight. I was scared but I learned how to hide my fear. However, as time went on, my fears actually diminished because assuming fearlessness taught me fearlessness.

In 1952, through my realization, I lost all fear. How nice that is!

I don't think I ever had any spiritual experiences when I was a boy. If anything, I was very much against all that nonsense.

In fact, I was strongly anti-religious. I even fought my parents on it, especially my father with his ideas of dietary law. I upset the kosherism of the house because I thought it nonsense.

We had a maid, and I got her to buy steaks at a non-kosher butcher store. Kosher steaks, being fresh, were tough, like leather. The non-kosher steaks were aged and tender.

As my father ate, he remarked how great the steaks were. I said, "you like them?"

He said, "They're excellent."

"Well," I said, "they're not kosher." He gave me a look and I thought he was going to tear me apart. He didn't say a word, he was so furious. But he didn't stop eating the steaks.

I shouldn't have done that. It showed the rebel in me at times.

The only reason we kept a kosher house was that my grandfather lived nearby. My grandfather and his father were holy, orthodox men.

I was given the usual early religious training until I was twelve.

When I entered college and began some deep thinking on that religious training I thought, "Gee, how they fooled me!" I rebelled and went the complete reverse. I was so anti-religious I used to mock God.

I remember once saying to my orthodox grandfather, "You cannot prove your God. What makes you believe in God?" And he answered, "All my life I have believed in Him. Now, near the end, should I take the change of not believing?" This made me aware of his broadmindedness and his love towards me.

## *LOVE IS TAKING PEOPLE AS THEY ARE*

The one person I really spoke to intimately while I was in high school was Si, a friend who was beyond me in years. He taught at Rutgers University, in Newark, the next town, and I really looked up to him as a guide.

You don't talk philosophically to a fellow who's of your own age. I was way beyond my years in what I was reading and studying. In grammar school I was studying the medical books of my father's aborted medical career, that he had around the house. And in high school I was reading psychology, economics and philosophy. So by the time I hit college, I was very deep into all these things.

Si really led me into the heart of all the philosophies—Kant, Hegel, Schopenhauer—I can't remember the other ones but I read them all very studiously and I understood them. We were also very interested in Freud and so we studied in a very intense manner—much better then you would in college—philosophy, psychology, economics, both of us seeking the answers.

He never got them. He thought the answer was economics until he eventually saw it wasn't, but he never saw what was.

But he was a guiding light, so to speak, for many, many years through high school, college days and postcollege days.

He's the one who liked camping and led me into it. We would spend the summer up in the Catskill Mountains, and occasionally in the Adirondack Mountains of New York State.

We had a beautiful community life of campers—quite a variation of types there. We had Mr. Coar who was a minister, a reverend. And we had Jack, taxicab driver, who was a real New York City rebel activist. And then we had Si who was the college professor and very philosophical. And there were others.

Each one would set up his own camp for himself and maybe another one. And in the evenings we'd get together around the campfire. We'd make our favorite, what we called slum gullion. We'd get a big washing pail—two-and-a-half gallons—and throw everything into it, beans, meats, salamis, spices, onions, vegetables and hot dogs. It would cook for hours and hours. And it really was delicious.

And often, after everyone went to bed, Si and I would talk deep into the night. We talked about all the philosophies and the "why's" of life. We discussed mainly the two major philosophical schools of idealism and materialism. We rejected agnosticism and getting nowhere. Then, I thought philosophy was the greatest means of understanding. Now, I see philosophy as nothing more than going in circles with words, as you do not get the understanding of life.

Materialism appealed to me then. The other seemed silly. I built such a beautiful, solid, concrete, materialistic philosophy that I thought it was unshakable. I could prove to you anything I would say. It was like the law of gravity. I'd hold a pencil and keep dropping it. It worked all the time. I'd say, "This is the law of gravity. Now prove to me your God. You can't. Therefore there is no God. It's nonsense."

In high school I became the intellectual type, interested in books and the so-called-better-things-in-life. Music interested me, especially jazz. I taught myself how to play the piano. I could really play jazz, didn't need notes. I could hear a tune and then play it.

I was good in all the sports. I played handball and tennis with the top winners in high school and college. And I could beat them, as long as it wasn't in competition. Competitively, I was no good. So I could never be on the teams.

I was graduated from high school in 1925. I was an honor student but always had the weird feeling every time I took an exam that I was going to fail. Instead I'd come out with the highest marks. This went on for 12 years! What anxiety and sweat I would go through before an exam! That was how little I thought of me. Isn't that what an inferiority complex is?

My marks in math and science, without studying, were always in the 90's. English and history I would just struggle through with 80's. I had no interest in them.

Anyone is smart in any subject he is interested in; anyone is dumb in any subject he is not interested in.

In high school, even though I had this inferiority complex which made me think myself unattractive, the girls used to say, "Oh, isn't he cute."

It's a funny thing to go through life being one way, and feeling the opposite all the time. The girls thought I was good-looking; I though I wasn't. It was a habitual belittling of myself.

I was intensely sexed and my whole life centered around sex. Wanting women made me—with tremendous effort—break through my shyness. I used to scheme, "How can I get them?" It was through observing that I learned to get the women I wanted.

And it worked out beautifully.

I used to watch what the other fellows did. I'd notice what the girls did and didn't like. The other fellows would throw out compliments so loosely that the girls knew it was just flattery and not real. I saw that girls liked compliments. Every girl had nice things about her. So I complimented them, but only on the things that were really true.

Also, I noticed the boys talked a lot about themselves; the girls didn't like that. They liked to be talked about. So I didn't talk about myself; I talked about them.

These things always got me the girl I wanted. Always.

I knew how to make a play for a girl and win; this, in spite of the tremendous obstacle of shyness. After I established rapport, then the shyness was no longer an obstacle; it was an asset. Girls loved it!

I looked up to, worshiped and idolized women, and therefore couldn't have anything to do with a prostitute, or some girl picked up on the street. I could never understand my college fraternity brothers saying they wouldn't dare touch their girlfriends—but they would go to bed with strange girls they picked up on the street, who in no way compared with their girlfriends.

Do you know why the fellows did that? That's what they thought of sex.

To me, sex was made for the girl you loved. That was so natural!

Sex brought out the finest emotions in me. I had the highest respect for women. Wanting to protect their reputations, I would never tell anyone of my affairs. In those days, for an unmarried women, having sex was committing the unpardonable sin.

Basically, sex brought out my finer feelings of love and really made me a giving person.

During those days, when people asked me if I believed in God, I would say, "Yes." And when they would ask, "What is your concept of God?" I would say, "Sex!" On their surprise, I would explain that it brought out in me the noblest and finest of human feelings, and that nothing could bring out these feelings as well as sex could.

Later I discovered that sex pegs your joy at that level and keeps you from increasing your joy. I've reached a state where now I always have more joy than what sex can give at its best. There is no limit to the joy that one may experience.

Even in grammar school I was always madly in love. Every grade I was in I fell in love with one beautiful girl. I remember the first one, Marcella Higgins in the first grade, Marcella Kahn in the second, Ethel Solomon in the third, and so on. Although I was so intensely enamored of them, they never knew it.

Ethel Solomon was seated right across the aisle from me. And every time she looked at me, I turned red. I almost died every time she'd speak to me. Shyness to the extreme.

Can you see what a torturous life I lived?

During my adolescent years, we had many parties. The fellows were always crude and forward with girls, so the girls ran away from them to me for protection, because I was nice!

Because of my shyness, I was never forceful with them—just the opposite. I really wanted to protect them, beside enjoying the pleasant feeling of being their hero.

Through protecting them, we got involved. It was natural.

I had sex all my life, never really promiscuously, but with many women, one at a time. I never cared to have more than one at a time. I wanted love with the girl I went to bed with.

I was in love and kept going with Annette in high school and halfway through college.

We had a good, healthy, natural sex relationship, the way it should be when two people are in love. When you're a teenager, sex is very intense.

I was going to Rutgers in New Brunswick, New Jersey while she was going to the University of Pennsylvania. We couldn't see each other because of distance. She started dating other fellows and over the phone she told me about it.

I was so extremely jealous it was tearing my insides apart. I couldn't take it. I almost flunked out that third year in college. I had to take a re-exam in my major. It was one term only, so I still made honors.

When I started college, dormitories were few, and I was rooming far off campus. Being against the idea of fraternities with their exclusiveness, I avoided them. However, the inconveniences of off-campus living were great. So I finally moved into a fraternity house, right on campus.

Living there gave me a very balanced collegiate life. I was a good student and also participated in all the social activities, attended all athletic events—even followed the football team around—and was very active in handball, tennis and swimming.

I loved college. It gave me avenues of freedom that made it easier for a shy person like myself to move into the world.

You suddenly became a man when you entered college. You moved out of your being-treated-like-a-child family into your own home, your fraternity house.

I was a man and we were men talking about important, big-time worldly subjects. Oh, we were smart! We knew more than our professors knew!

We talked about the world and women, played cards, often until the sun came up. Then we'd go to bed to get an hour or two sleep before eight o'clock class.

I remember the glamour of college in those days. "Rah, Rah, Rutgers. I'll die for dear old Rutgers!" The whole thing was Hollywoodian naive—fairytaleish!

At that time, usually only the sons of rich men went to college. I never considered myself one of them. Although my father started me, I had to finish by working my way through.

I went to work during the third year of college when I got a letter which said, "Dear Lester, I can't send any more money. Love, Dad." The Depression had broken him financially.

I thought that my world had come to an end, as I equated my college education to my world. I even considered suicide, which was a thought that would reoccur to me on occasion until 1952.

It took me three days to figure out I could work my way through college! Immediately I got a dual job in the fraternity house in which I was living, washing dishes and stoking the coal furnace. That partly took care of me. A few months later, I managed to get a real position as a laboratory assistant in the physics department.

I always felt poor. Compared to the other fellows, I was. My roommate's father was a millionaire—in the thirties! But it didn't bother me that they were rich. It bothered me that I felt poor.

We didn't differentiate in the fraternity house. We were frat brothers, and naturally we worked for one another. We felt like one happy family, freed from parental oppression.

I rebelled against compulsory daily chapel.

We had to go to chapel every day. Some of the fellows would take decks of cards and play while the poor chaplain gave the sermon. There was so much talking that no one could hear him. I felt sorry for him. But we won our point; chapel was changed to Sundays only, and voluntary.

They were giving us the usual organized religious teaching, which doesn't go far enough. When you're in college and you're young, you're thinking, and you can see how silly the stuff is they're pouring out to you.

Rebellion came out in our day also in the form of our dress. We wore raccoon coats and derby hats! What an odd combination. But such things always went on, and go on today.

Youth always objects. Youth rebels, not knowing really what they're against. It is simply non-freedom.

R.O.T.C. was compulsory and I protested military training. I was anti-military, and was the worst soldier in the worst company.

We were given old World War I uniforms. They were heavy wool and itchy. My jacket was too short and pants were too long. With my jacket buttoned, I could just about breathe. My pants looked like bloomers. My boy-scout-looking hat set on top of my head. I looked like a real Hollywood comic.

I liked this comic dress. It fit in with my attitude about the military.

Drill was where I could express the way I felt. I'd play dumb. They'd command, "Right, march!" and I'd go left.

One time at drill our officer, a recent graduate from West Point, wanted to give us a rest. He had us stack our rifles and went into a speech emphasizing the point of not going near the stacked arms: "Stay away from the arms. When you break ranks, don't move through the stacks. Move back away from them. Stay away from them. And remember, don't touch the arms!"

As he said that, I instinctively put my arm out to touch a stack, thinking he wouldn't see me. But at that moment his head swung around and he saw me touch it. I quickly pulled my hand back. But unfortunately, the stack of rifles had been wrongly stacked, and down it went, hitting the next stack, which hit the next one.

Did the officer have it in for me! He was so furious that he huffed and he puffed. He just couldn't say a word to me.

I got a big share of demerits for that.

The two West Point graduates who were in charge called me in for a conference after the second year, at the end of the course. They told me they were going to flunk me. They said that although my class marks were in the 90s, my drill work had so many demerits that I would have to take the last year over again.

I thought it over. Then I pointed my finger at them and said, "Okay, remember. You fellows flunk me, and you're going to have me another year!"

They looked at each other and then said, "You're passed!"

I was a wise guy. I knew the military wouldn't do anything to me in peacetime. They didn't have a guardhouse!

## *LOVE AND UNDERSTANDING ARE THE SAME*

I graduated from Rutgers in 1931 at the age of twenty-two.

I wanted to be the greatest physicist in the world, but I couldn't get a job. The very few physicists working in those days had been laid off. Still I felt as though I was going to conquer the world. I never let up seeking work. I was turned down day in and day out, but I never stopped looking.

Since I couldn't get a job as a physicist, I decided to go into engineering. Physics was the basis for all engineering, and as extra study I had taken electrical and mechanical engineering. I had also taken the required educational courses to qualify for a teaching certificate.

So I came out of college qualified for several things.

My first job with an aeronautical engineer lasted only three months because they went out of business.

Then I looked for work as a teacher.

Jobs being so hard to get, I would go every day to the superintendent of schools' office and ask him for a job. Week in and week out, I was doing this, until one day—I believe in order to get rid of me—he gave me a job substituting for a man who had a class of incorrigibles. These boys had already been expelled from school for having done violent things, and were on their way to reform school. This class was an attempt to possibly bring some of the boys back into the school system rather than send them on to the reform school.

Wanting a job so badly, I was happy to be given this work. However, on the way into the school, Jacques Street School, Number Nine, I met the supervisor of physical education for the city, Mr. Allison, my old gym teacher from Battin High. When I told him where I was headed, he said, "Don't go in there. If I were you, I wouldn't do it. Yesterday they took the substitute teacher before you, and actually threw him over the fence. And he's bigger than you. Stay away."

I was so determined and so wanting work, I said, "I'll try it anyway." With my learned fearlessness, I dared the assignment.

I walked into the class—they were in their carpentry shop—and it was pandemonium. One kid was sawing his desk in half, another was chopping plaster out of the wall with a hammer, and every other one was doing anything and everything that he wanted to do.

So I went up to the boy sawing his desk in half and told him to stop it. He just looked at me and turned around as though I weren't there.

I went to the boy chopping plaster out of the wall and asked him to stop. He answered, "Go to hell!"

I went to the front of the class, I picked up a plank—a four-inch-wide plank about three feet long—and yelled out, like a thunder clap, "Quiet!"

However no one paid any attention to it, except for just a moment.

I went for the fellow sawing his desk in half, hit him and he stopped.

Then I went for the fellow who was chopping the plaster out of the wall and he started running, but I caught him in the back. I didn't hurt him much.

What I was doing gave me the attention of the class. So I went back to the front of the class, and again yelled, "Quiet!" Then something started that I was concerned might happen: the leader of the class, stood up and said, "Okay boys, let him—" and before he could say the words "have it" I went for him. With both my hands on the plank, I came down over his head and he fell back into his seat, stunned. Fortunately, the plank broke in half, which allowed me a better grip on it.

Then I went for a second fellow who had moved to join him. He started to run away. But I swung at him and cut four of his fingers. For me it was do or die. I was really in there ready to take on the whole class.

From that spot, I yelled, "Okay! Who's next?" Then as a group, the whole class sat down in their seats. They submitted to my challenge and became absolutely quiet.

I then opened the door and soon Miss Kellog, the principal, peeked in. She looked stunned. I said, "Come in, Miss Kellog." When she did, she couldn't talk. She had expected to find me in pieces, but I was fine and the kids were perfectly still. I said, "Everything is fine." She stuttered something and walked out, a little dazed.

This all happened in the first minutes of my coming into the class. For the rest of the week I had excellent rapport with the boys, much more so than I believed, because at the end of the last day with the class I said to them, "Mr. Peters will be back tomorrow," and they all exclaimed in unison, "Aw-w-w." I said, "What's the matter?"

"Oh, we like you. We wish you'd stay!"

This puzzled me at first. Then I realized the reason for it was I was talking to them in the language they understood. I was talking to them at their level. I was not hitting them out of blood-thirstiness. I wasn't even wanting to hit them.

I had guts and they liked that. I was able to communicate better than I realized because I understood them. I was given the job of being the leader, the teacher. They were challenging it. I took the challenge and showed them that I could be the leader. This they understood and this they accepted, and this they liked.

I was telling them, "Look, this is my job. I've been given the position of being the leader here. You fellows shouldn't, and can't take it away from me. If you do, I'll do whatever is necessary to re-establish my leadership here."

You couldn't have a class with you unless you were with it, unless you had a feel for it, unless you had love for your pupils. A teacher who had hatred for a class couldn't control it.

Because of my ability to communicate, the kids were with me. I got the reputation of being a good disciplinarian. I was told I would lose my job if I hit the kids, but I did it anyway. It was necessary, I thought, for control.

It's interesting how my students reacted. I once lost my temper and swung a blackboard pointer at a boy as he was running away. I caught him across the forehead and forearm, and he developed two welts.

The next day in school he came to me and said, "Gee, Mr. Levenson, my old man beat the hell outta me, wanting me to tell him who did this to me. But I wouldn't."

He protected me.

That wild experience with the thirty "incorrigible" boys earned me respect and my first regular teaching assignment. I taught geometry to juniors and seniors in the high school I had graduated from. Battin High had been made an all girls high school. I was twenty-two, teaching girls who were eighteen! It was humiliating.

Because of my extreme shyness, the girls would tease me by coming up after class and crowding around me, pushing against me. I'd squirm, and they knew I was squirming.

Some would sit purposely letting their dresses go above their knees. And I'd have to look away.

I used to walk home from school, as I lived only a half mile away. Some of the girls with cars would slow down and shout to me, "Yoo-hoo, would you like to have a ride?"

“No, thank you,” I’d say, hoping the principal or another teacher saw it. They teased the life out of me.

Jobs being very scarce, I wanted to hold that position. I couldn’t risk having the principal or anyone else see anything that didn’t look perfectly respectable for a teacher.

At the end of the teaching year, the teacher that I had replaced returned and I was sent to a junior high school in the poorest section of Elizabethport, New Jersey. I was given the most difficult kids to work with, the group with the lowest I.Q.

It was a weird thing, that experience of teaching. In a way I was rough with the kids, but I never had the attitude that I was their superior. I dealt with them person to person. My attitude was one of understanding them and what they were doing, and behaving accordingly. Understanding and love are the same.

They certainly protected me. They could have had me thrown out of the school system again and again for hitting them, and they knew it. But they never did.

You see, it is not what you do, but your attitude as you do it that counts.

During the second year of teaching I grew tired of it and quit. It was dull. I wanted to be a scientist. There were no jobs. I was frustrated and I was confused. I felt heavy, heavy all over.

## *ONE DOES NOT INCREASE HIS LOVE ONE MERELY GETS RID OF ONE'S HATE*

About the middle of the Depression I had no job so I went camping for the summer. I loved camping. It was the nicest recreation I knew. For many years, working or not working, I'd take the summer off and go camping. I'd just throw up a piece of canvas and bed under it. I usually camped with one or two others.

We caught fish by hand. Belly-tickling, it was called. It was illegal, but the fastest way of catching fish. I'd feel under the rocks for speckled brook trout. While under the rock, the fish thinks your hand is part of the environment floating by, and feels safe. Once I made contact, I worked my hand up toward the fish's head, grabbed it tightly, and quickly threw it on the bank as it was slipping out of my grasp.

But there was a twenty-five dollar fine for each fish, so we'd fish in twos. One of us would watch out for the game warden. Each time we'd catch a fish, we'd hide it and get another one. In a matter of minutes, we got a meal together that way.

I loved to live naturally. We tried to live off the land, eating the apples and berries that grew wild in the Catskills and the corn, vegetables and milk that the farmers sometimes gave us. We even drank milk warm from the cow, although it had an odor and didn't taste good, thinking that was natural.

My camping was an escape from the world. Every time I'd go camping, in a day or two all my pains and ulcers would disappear; when I'd get back to the city, in a few days my sicknesses would return.

One summer, I camped in the Catskills. I arrived at camp late at night dead tired. Fred was arguing with four of the other fellows about some girl Virginia. They were all agog about her. The argument kept going on and I wanted to sleep. So I said, "Fred, will you shut the hell up and go to sleep?"

"Aw, keep quiet, Levenson, you haven't got a chance anyhow."

Well, that was a challenge and I always responded to a challenge. So I jumped up out of bed and said, "What do you mean I don't have a chance! She's my girl."

It ended with only Fred and I arguing. Fred said, "Well, I want to marry her!" He thought that would shut me up.

So I stopped that by saying, "Well, I want to marry her, too!" In the arguing he had forgotten that I hadn't even met her yet.

And then Fred in a gallant, dramatic gesture stuck his hand out and said, "Well, let the best man win." And we shook hands on that. I thought to myself, "Thank God! Now I can go to sleep."

The next morning when I got up, stacks and stacks of dishes, unwashed, were piled around the kitchen area. Things were as dirty as disorganized as they could be. I got disgusted and I said, "I can't stay here. I'll camp with two fellows I know a few miles up the road in Oliverea."

So I took off for Oliverea. When I went back to get my things, on the way there was a very attractive girl hitchhiking towards Big Indian where the boys were. I picked her up and when I got to the bridge where I had to turn left, I said, "Well, I'm going left here."

She said, "Well, that's all right. I'm going left."

Then a quarter of a mile, and I said, "I'm going left here."

She said, "Fine. I'm going left."

I got to the driveway and said, "I'm going in here."

She said, "Well, that's where I'm going."

I said, "Where are you going?"

She said, "I'm going to visit the boys at the camp."

I said, "Oh. That's where I'm going."

And so, there I drive in with Virginia.

Of course, Freddy and Kessle said, "That son of a gun. What a double crosser he is! Says he's going to camp in Oliverea and he sneaks out and picks her up."

The battle was on. Immediately they started making wisecrack remarks about me. Then Freddie said, "Ah, I know what he's doing. He's playing on her sympathy." So he led all the fellows in singing that song, "Sympathy."

And that got me furious.

I said to myself, "This is it. I'm going all out." I wasn't really terribly interested in her. She seemed artificial. But the challenge and what they were doing made me determined.

I used the old head. Well, she lived in Oliverea so I had an advantage in that. Next she had a girl friend, Midge, who was one of the most brilliant girls you could ever meet. But she was as homely as she was brilliant. Luckily, her father was a wealthy doctor so she had the money to overcome the looks with unusually smart clothes. Virginia was jealous of Midge's mind. And Midge was jealous of Virginia's looks.

I made a play for Midge only to get Virginia.

And it worked.

But before that, one day Freddie invited Virginia to camp. She asked me for a lift. I said, "Sure."

Virginia and I drove into the camp where Fred and the boys were. As I parked the car, Fred immediately got in on the other side and started making a strong play for Virginia. I let it go on, I had no choice. I kept quiet until he said, "Oh, I think love is one of the most wonderful things."

Then I said, "Fred, you are so right!" And I leaned over and put both my arms around Virginia and gave her a real warm kiss and held her tightly.

Fred almost died.

Virginia was floored because I really was not at that time that close to her. I had known her only a few days. After the incident was over, I told Virginia what I was doing. She didn't like it. She liked the attention of men and I was upsetting her chances with the boys.

Virginia was a beautiful girl, and an artist. She outdid Hollywood sophistication. We became very close.

I was awfully nice to Virginia. I'd do anything and everything for her—except marry her. Poetry, flowers, moonlight swimming together!

I fell in love. But because I wouldn't marry her, she later left me. That was rough.

But the mountains! Up there it was heavenly! So ideal. No worries, no cares. Pure romance, swimming, handball, tennis, dancing at night, nature.

It doesn't sound as though I had such a miserable life, does it, when I talk about that summer?

Ah, but what agonies when we were breaking up! One beautiful summer and a broken heart for years.

I had an unconscious fear of getting tied up in marriage that was so strong it prevented me from ever marrying. Because I felt so bound up all the time I feared marriage would put a big increase on that non-freedom I was feeling.

I tried once to force marriage with an awfully nice girl from Elizabeth. This was toward the beginning of World War II.

President Roosevelt had signed the draft act. I thought, "Well, I might go to war and be killed. I should get married and leave some offspring."

So I said to Selma, point blank, "Would you like to get married?"

"Yes!" she said.

I said, "Okay, would you go down to the state of Virginia with me right now?"

She said, "Yes."

So we took off for Virginia where you can get married right away. All the way down I couldn't talk. After driving a couple of hours, I swallowed hard and with a gulp asked, "Are you hungry?"

And she said, "Yes."

"Okay, we'll eat."

Throughout the meal I couldn't talk. I felt as though I were Atlas with the whole weight of the world on my back. But I was determined to go through with it.

We crossed the Virginia state line and stopped at the first place with a sign "Marriages Performed Immediately."

A minister came out and said, "Oh, you'd like to get married? Fine."

When he said, "Fine," I blacked out for a moment.

Then he said, "Now, you have to take a place in town and stay three days before I can do this. The new law requires that."

I saw my way out. "Oh! In that case, I can't wait because I must be back for work." It really was no excuse, it blurted out uncontrolled. I felt as though the world had rolled off my back.

I just couldn't go through with it.

On the way home not a word was said.

After this incident I never saw Selma again. I was just too ashamed. I wanted to see her. But I just couldn't.

The marriage obstacle was unconscious then. Now, of course, I know what it was. Unconsciously I wanted freedom so much that I couldn't allow myself the tie of marriage.

## *TO LOVE OUR ENEMY IS THE HEIGHT OF LOVE*

After that summer, and the break-up with Virginia, I decided to go abroad and escape from my unhappy world. The Depression was on and everything was so difficult. I was terribly unhappy and frustrated at the way my life was working out.

One hundred and twenty-five dollars bought me a roundtrip ticket to Liverpool, England, and launched me on a period of freedom from my inner extreme frustration, tensions and anxieties. I spent most of the time abroad in Helsinki.

It was such an ideal, quiet, clean city! And the rate of exchange was so favorable. I'd get hundreds of their marks for one dollar. On three dollars a week, I had everything I needed.

For that period I just lived. I had saved enough money from teaching.

I did nothing but observe. The nicest thing was the escape from me and my miseries. Here I was in a strange country, strange ways, language—everything different. It fascinated me and incidentally broadened me. I saw that what was right conduct in one country was often wrong in another. This taught me greater acceptance of all peoples and their ways. I believe I gained more of a practical knowledge of living and people by traveling than I had learned in four years of college.

I personally felt that traveling was the very nicest way of entertaining myself. Next to traveling, it was camping out in nature.

Even in Europe I always found a girl, and lived similarly as I did in America.

I came back from Europe in 1935 and sought a job as an air conditioning engineer. I thought air conditioning was the coming thing. It was just starting about that time.

I applied for a job and was told by Kelvinator that they didn't need another engineer. I told them I'd work for nothing, and actually offered my services free.

They started me and in a week or two paid me fifteen dollars a week. It didn't take long before I was getting fifty dollars a week. For that time it was excellent pay. I soon tired of the work and quit before the year was up. I figured out that I could sell at Kelvinator's cost and make their mark-up by going into business on my own. I used the address and phone number of a friend who was clerking in a legal office. My office was in my hat. I was my own salesman, engineer, installation man, electrician, plumber and serviceman.

The first job I installed in 1937 in the Red Cross Shoe store. When I put the job in, I did it in the way I knew would be the very best. I slowed the fan and slightly over-sized the equipment. I knew it would last.

When I was selling the job, the store owner asked, "How do I know this is going to work? Two thousand dollars is a lot of money, you know."

I had an idea. I said, "If it doesn't work, you don't pay me! Just let me put it in, but sign the contract now."

I knew that with his signature I could borrow money from the bank next door. To put the job in.

I installed it, it worked well, and he paid for it.

That started me off in the air conditioning business. I discovered I could work four months a year and make more than I made as an engineer working a whole year.

That was at the time my father died and left a luncheonette business with a ten-thousand-dollar indebtedness. So I ran the air conditioning business and the luncheonette at the same time. I just wanted to pay off the family debts and dump the luncheonette. That's what I did.

I was restless and bored. I thought I would hit the big town, New York City. I dropped New Jersey and went to New York in 1938 with a smart idea. I opened up a very small and very efficient luncheonette called the Hitching Post. It was the smallest restaurant in New York, so said a newspaper—eleven seats around a circular counter.

I designed the counter out of ash wood and an old craftsman from Germany hand made the stools. They were beautiful so much more beautiful than the usual chrome and red plastic furniture of those days. The walls were mahogany. The whole place had a natural air of wood, with a fireplace in a corner.

I really engineered the food business. I was able to get the prices very low and the percentage profits very high.

We sold a hot roast beef sandwich on a warm soft roll dipped in natural gravy for ten cents, and a hot Virginia ham sandwich on a warm soft roll dipped in natural gravy for ten cents. Our home-made buttercrust apple pie was baked on the premises, and a la mode or with a slice of cheese, the price was ten cents. The pie was really delicious.

Although these prices were very low, the percentage profit was much higher than the majority of eating places.

By 1941 I had three Hitching Post restaurants going and a fourth was underway. I was making twelve hundred dollars a week and, at the time, living in the Hotel Taft on Broadway, New York City.

I used to work twelve to fourteen hours a day—around the clock—seven days a week. I always worked long hours—for two reasons: first, because I always started in business with no money; second, I need the difficult involvement to escape from my turbulent, unhappy mind.

Then the war interfered.

In July 1941 I was called in as an engineer for U.S. Maritime Commission in Washington, D.C. They needed ships to deliver the war material to England. I worked in the engineering plan approval division, on ships piping and machinery.

From the start of this job I always had the thought of leaving it and returning full time to the restaurants. However, I was locked into my job. Because of the war, I could not leave my employment. I was considered necessary to the war effort so they sent a deferment to my draft board.

Every Saturday afternoon at 1 p.m. I left Washington for New York, to look after the Hitching Posts; every Sunday night at 7 p.m. I'd drive back to Washington, 470 long miles, roundtrip.

But I couldn't operate them from afar, and I lost all the Hitching Post restaurants.

At the Maritime Commission I was surprised to meet strong anti-Semitism amongst my fellow engineers.

When I first walked into the Commission, an elderly engineer said, "Come here." I walked over to him. He asked me if I were a Jew. When I told him, he said, "Well, I hate all Jews."

"Why?" I asked.

"Well, all Jews are crooks," he answered.

"Are you calling me a crook?" I asked.

"Well, all Brooklyn Jews are crooks," he replied. So I answered, "I come from Brooklyn," although I really didn't. He just turned away and wouldn't talk with me anymore.

That was my introduction to the Maritime Commission. My blood used to boil when confronted with anti-Semitism but I suppressed the anger, at least outwardly.

At another time, one of my co-workers came up to me and said, “Oh, I got this thing in one of your stores.”

I said, “What do you mean?” I didn’t have any stores in Washington.

“I got gypped,” he said.

“One of my stores?” I inquired again.

“You know, I bought it in a Jew-store.”

That was the way it went, again and again, with my fellow engineers.

While working for Kelvinator as an engineer in 1936, the senior engineer said to me one day, “You know, Lester, before I met you I thought all Jews and niggers were the same. But now I think the Jews are a little bit better.”

These are not special incidents. This sort of thing went on all my life until I gained my freedom and realized that I was responsible for everything that was happening to me. Then it stopped.

I was beat up when I was a kid for being a Jew. In high school I was often ostracized and attacked. In college I joined a Jewish fraternity. The fellows I played touch football with in non-Jewish fraternity across the street wouldn’t talk to me if they met me at a college dance.

I got this kind of treatment continuously all my life until 1952. I'd hear remarks all the time, everywhere, on the streets. I was never away from it.

When jobs were extremely scarce and I needed work, I was first accepted and then turned down by the Manhattan Project because I was a Jew. That was the project to develop the atomic bomb. I never was sorry about that one.

I was classified 2B. Humorously, I though that means to be here when they go and to be here when they come back.

2B meant essential to the war effort. Engineers especially were very needed to produce the goods. So that got me a deferment right through the war, although I was tied in as tightly as any man in uniform. All my bosses were in uniform and were either generals or near-generals. I had no freedom to move around. I had to go where they sent me. So in a way it was like being in the Army without being in a uniform.

When I saw some of my fellow workers, who also had deferments, being drafted, I thought, "Well, one of these days I'll have to go."

But I couldn't get myself to the place where I could kill. I just felt that I could never kill a man.

But then I said, "Well, I'll have to kill. I might get to the front line." So I began training myself so that in case I were drafted, I'd be able to kill. I used to read all the Nazi atrocities to the Jews and I'd imagine myself as being one of them.

But even though I kept doing this for months, I still ended up with the feeling that I couldn't kill.

I said, "Well, if I have to, maybe I'll close my eyes and do it."

In 1943 I was shifted to Philadelphia. There I got fed up with ships and pipes, and worked my way into the U.S. Engineers working out of 120 Wall Street, getting up plans and specifications for construction at army installations. I had gotten back home to New York City! That was my plan.

But through all this period, I was sick mentally with anxieties and depression, sick physically with ulcers, hay fever, gastro-intestinal imbalances and migraine headaches.

While I was in Washington I had begun to develop fears of going under a bridge or into a building, thinking they might collapse on me. Even though rationally I knew they couldn't, I couldn't get rid of the fear. I was forcing myself to go under railroad bridges.

This made me think I was going insane. And when you think you're going insane, you really get scared! It drove me to seek a way out. I went into the study of Freud with intensity.

Then I went into psychoanalysis. Four years of it—four times a week—under a former associate of Sigmund Freud. In 1946 I was discharged with the comment that some people cannot be helped.

It had done me no good.

## *WHEN ONE REALLY LOVES ONE CAN NEVER BE HURT*

After being turned away by my analyst I went my usual way.

When the war ended, having been a marine engineer for two years and a construction engineer for three years, I looked for a good business to get into. There was a dire shortage of homes, and lumber was hard to get. So I decided on the lumber business.

I never had money when I started a business. I always had to work on ideas. Money does not make money. Ideas make money.

A planing mill in Canada charged three dollars a thousand board feet; in the States, the cost was ten dollars. Seven dollars was the normal profit per thousand feet. That made it a good business.

I got into my car and drove to Canada. For one dollar, I rented all the space around a planing mill in St. Raymond, about thirty miles out of Quebec City. In return, the owner of the planing mill would get all my business. I arranged for the sawmillers in the area to air-dry their timber there.

I got another fellow to work for me and handle the New York office which was my apartment on 225 West 23rd Street. We'd sell the lumber in the New York-New Jersey area, and he'd take orders and take care of the customers.

In Canada I'd have the planning mill take the lumber from the stacks of drying lumber, put it through a belt line through the planer into a railroad car.

The mill owner would seal the car, write out a bill of lading, hand it to me, and I would give him a check for the lumber and the planing of it.

I'd air mail the bill of lading to my man in New York. He'd run to the customer, get the customer's check, then deposit it to cover mine.

I got up to shipping two carloads of lumber a day and I was making three hundred dollars a carload. I could have made four or five hundred a carload, but I was satisfied with three.

Very early in this business, a customer left on vacation and was gone for several weeks. That could've wrecked me as I needed his check to cover mine for the two carloads I had just shipped to him. I always had good credit but I was a stranger in Canada and one check bouncing would have ruined me. A carload averaged $2500 and I had a $5000 check that had to be covered.

I immediately took an airplane back to New York City and asked two or three banks for a loan to cover my lumber. They asked what security I had, and I told them—none. I didn't get the loan.

I had to cover that $5000 check or lose the business I'd just started. I remembered from the past how my confidence would flow over to the one I was speaking to. I figured I was lacking confidence. So I took two days off to develop it. I would bring up the feeling of confidence and strengthen this feeling until it just oozed out of me. Then I had it.

I walked into a strange bank, the Trade Bank and Trust Company, on Seventh Avenue and 34th Street. I knew they were dealing with the big lumber companies and I figured they'd understand lumber.

I wanted to see the president, but he was away on vacation. "Well, in that case," I said, "I'll see the VP."

They introduced me to him, the toughest guy in the bank. I knew I was going to get the loan. I never deviated from that.

He asked many questions and I answered them. "All right," he said, "Come in tomorrow. I think I'll give it to you."

I went in the next day and he started asking more questions. I could see he did not want to give me the loan.

He asked, "Did you say this?"

I said, "No, I said this." He was asking me about some very positive things that I had been thinking but had not voiced. I knew I had not said them. Yet he had picked them up! I thought it was very weird. To me mind reading was all nonsense in those days.

In the middle of his questioning he stood up, reached over, grabbed my hand in both of his and said, "Be careful, just be careful, I'm letting you have it."

My security for the loan was the invoice. I would invoice the customer, assign the invoice to the bank, and the bank would give me eighty percent of the invoice, which covered all my costs. Ten thousand dollars credit was granted. That got me going again—just in time. It took about six to eight days to clear a check, and now my check was covered.

Here's another strange incident. One time I wanted to make a good buy in lumber and needed $4000 cash. I was in St. Raymond, Quebec at the time. I walked into the Royal Bank, wrote out a personal check for $4000 on my New York bank and handed it to the cashier to cash. She called over the manager and he asked me, "What do you want it for?"

"I want to buy lumber." I said.

He simply replied, "Okay," and gave me the cash. As I walked out of the bank I thought how weird this situation was—I, a stranger, was walking out of the door with $4000 cash in my pocket!

I went back and asked the manager why he had given me the cash so readily. I said, "You know I can walk out of this door and you could be out $4000." He said, "I'm not afraid."

I said, shaking his hand vigorously, "Thank you. You're a hundred percent safe. You'll never be hurt." And I walked out.

A stranger in a strange country—in a bank that I had not been in before—I wrote out a personal check for $4000. Trying to understand things like that used to give me a headache, so I would drop thinking about it. I said to myself,

"The confidence in me goes over to him. But what makes him so trusting, I cannot understand."

I always got credit and I always paid back.

As I was buying direct from sawmillers and by-passing the Canadian brokers, it didn't take long for the brokers to gang up on me. I was the only American by-passing them and getting lumber they couldn't get. I paid the sawmillers more, so I got the first choice on the lumber.

I had started this way: I met a Canadian sawmiller who had twelve or fourteen kids. I asked why he let his kids run around in the winter without shoes. He broke down and cried, and said he didn't earn enough money to buy his kids shoes. The Canadian brokers were cruel to the sawmillers. They wouldn't let them make a living, even when lumber was as valuable as gold.

I told the miller that I'd give him three dollars more per thousand feet for his lumber. It was the normal profit he should've been making. After that, naturally, I got all the lumber I wanted from him and all the other sawmillers.

I had accumulated about $80,000 worth of inventory when the Canadian brokers got after me.

They filed a charge against me for trying to leave the country while owing them $15,000. They did it late on a

Friday afternoon, knowing that I wouldn't have time to get a bond before Monday.

The judge ordered me to jail until the bond was posted. I was so furious that I held on to the bars with such strength that the jailer couldn't push me into the cell. We were locked in a struggle.

A lawyer, who happened to be there, saw what was going on, felt sympathy for me, and vouched for me. I was released on his recognizance. After that I made him one of my attorneys.

While the court case was on a stranger, who worked in the court, came up to me and said, "You know, you're going to win the case, but they're going to refile the same charge for $50,000."

I quickly saw my lawyer and he told me that I'd have to go to court for every charge and prove my innocence. The brokers had a scheme to keep me continuously tied up.

I knew I was licked. Before the verdict came out, I went home, packed my things, and flew to New York to gather myself and make a decision as what to do next.

The owner of the planing mill was a good fellow, so before I left I said to him, "Look, you take care of my things. There's a lot of money here, about $80,000 in lumber that I've paid for. Fight this out in court for me." He agreed.

It took many years of court actions until the court ordered the lumber sold to pay costs. I lost everything. I zeroed again.

## *ANYTIME ONE FEELS GOOD, ONE IS LOVING*
## *ANYTIME ONE FEELS BAD, ONE IS NOT LOVING*

Losing businesses seemed to be a habit with me, but that didn't stop me. A week after I left Canada I flew to San Francisco looking for lumber in northern California. I was there for only a few weeks when I was informed that there was a good deal in New Mexico. Within a week I landed in Albuquerque.

I bought a sawmill and a planing mill for one dollar. The mills were in debt for almost $100,000 and the bank had foreclosed them. The bank sold them to me for one dollar with my promise that I'd pay off the bank first, and then the labor.

I never had been in that business before. But here I was with an opportunity to get lumber, a scarce commodity, right at the source—the tree.

The sawmill was in Datil. The planing mill was very large, covering about half a mile alongside the railroad in Magdalena, with huge trucks, conveyors and equipment. I soon had a tremendous operation going, and I liked the bigness of it.

I started up the operation, managed to pay off all the debts—then the market for lumber collapsed! More than half of the post-war business was in the hands of small sawmillers like me. So the two biggest moguls had gotten together and suddenly dropped prices below our costs.

I had millions of board feet of paid-for lumber cut and drying, and owing the bank about $150,000 on it. I sold it for less than it cost me, paid off the bank, and ended up with nothing.

I was left with some old lumber, so I decided to build homes with it. I got a commitment for twelve homes from the Federal Housing Administration guaranteeing $100,000 of mortgages. All I needed was to own the land I wanted to build on. For next to nothing I was able to get title to enough land.

I did a beautiful job on those houses, as though I was going to live in them myself. The town fathers were selling similar houses for $12,500; I was selling them for $8,000, and still making $1,500 per house.

Labor was working then at forty cents an hour. I said to the men, "I'll start you at eighty cents an hour and if you're good I'll give you a dollar. If you're not, I'll let you go." I didn't realize that I was spoiling the local low-cost labor market.

So the town fathers went for me.

They sent Leslie to get me. He had been discharged from the army as a mental case. He entered my kitchen through the back door, sat on the edge of the kitchen table and told me that I had to leave town. When I refused, he pulled out a forty-five pistol, steadied his hand on the table with his finger on the trigger and as he said, "I'm going to let you have it," my eyes focused on his trigger finger and I thought, "Is this true? Can I be killed? Maybe he'll miss or just hit me on the shoulder."

As he began to squeeze the trigger I said to myself, "This is impossible! It can't be!"

Immediately on that thought there was a sudden loud rapping on the front door. Leslie, startled, stopped his action and ordered me to go into the living room, answer the door and tell the party, "I'm busy."

I opened the door, and as I started to say, "I'm busy " my next door neighbor, not listening to me, brushed me aside, walked into the kitchen, exclaimed to Leslie, "What are you doing with that gun?" and took it away from him.

I never could understand what impelled him to come in the nick of time, nor could he tell me more than just, "I had a feeling to come in."

Being a strong defender and a fighter for principle I said to myself, "I'm going to throw the legal book at that guy." But then I figured, "Hell, he's got two kids and a wife." So I went to him and said, "Les, I'm forgetting about that incident." He was so relieved that he grabbed me by the hand, shaking it and exclaiming, "Thank you, Thank you."

Then Manuel got after me. He entered my home and said, "If you don't give me $600 for the masonry work I've done, I'm going to beat you up." The job was worth only $50.

Manuel was a big bruiser and he had another even taller and tougher friend with him. This was rough country.

I said, "You can go to hell!" The two of them started for me, and as they did, I got an idea.

I held my hand to stop them and said, “Okay, I’ll give you the money.” I sat down and wrote out a check for $600.

The moment they left, I called the bank and stopped payment on the check.

Then I got into my car and drove to the bank. As I reached the entrance they were coming out. I yelled, “Ha, Ha, Ha,” right in their faces. I knew they wouldn’t do anything in public.

Manuel said, “You son-of-a-bitch! I’m going to get you. You wait.”

After that I thought, “If he tried it one time, he could do it again. I’d better do something.” So I went up to the college of mining in town where I knew a student who had a fast repeater pistol, a P-38, and I borrowed it. From another friend I borrowed a rifle.

Later Manuel and his buddy came back. I met them outside my home and pulled the pistol on them.

“If I ever see you guys within seeing distance, I’m going to kill you!” I said.

The taller one said, “Oh, you’re pretty big with a gun.”

I answered, “Big enough to kill you right now,” as I aimed for his head and pretended I was pulling the trigger. His legs buckled but he caught himself from falling. I was under full control at the time and kept my cool.

They went away scared. They bothered me no more.

When I went into my bedroom, saw the rifle by my bed, the pistol in my hand, I said to myself, "What the hell is going on here, Lester? Are you mad? You're not a gunman. What am I doing?"

All this was during the time that I was on phenobard to knock out the migraine headaches, and dexadrene sulphate to keep me going. I had to drink every weekend to escape the so heavy world, to be able to face it again on Monday morning. I really was down, down.

Looking at the guns, I made the decision right there and then to get out. What the hell was I doing here? My friends and family were back East.

I packed up, pulled out of the area and headed East.

I arrived in New York and immediately got overbusy. Not only did I start two miners working a lead mining claim in Belin, New Mexico, but at the same time raised funds and started drilling for oil in Kentucky. The work load and my anxieties culminated in a coronary thrombosis.

This extremity was the turning point in my life.

# *Second*

## Freedom

## *LOVE ELIMINATES FEAR*

## *LOVE IS THE ULTIMATE*

I was told by the doctor not to exert myself, that I must live a sedentary life, because I could drop dead at any moment. This scared me almost to death! After several days I said to myself, "I'm still alive! Drop this useless fear and instead use all you've got to see what you can do about it."

I resolved that either I get the answers or I'll take me off this earth, that no coronary was going to do it. And I had the where-with-all, enough morphine to do it—and in the most pleasant way. The doctors allowed me to have morphine to use when I would be overtaken by a kidney-stone attack.

The major thing I did after my coronary thrombosis was cut out from the world, one hundred percent. Formerly, I had been very active socially in the arts, opera, jazz, ballet and theatre, whenever I was in New York. It was my necessity for escape.

However, for three months I stopped all social activity, did no dating, and even cut out the weekend visits to my sisters and their families. I also cut off the phone.

It was a total cut-out from the world. I isolated, right in New York City. I'd only go out to buy food between 2 and 5 A.M. when the city streets were the emptiest. Stores were open all night in Manhattan. I saw no one except the grocer.

I was all out, hellbent on getting the answers.

I had spent over forty years of my life, mostly very unhappily. Friends would tell me, "Gee, Lester, you've got everything." I felt I had nothing.

I had a nice family and an unusually loving mother. I was given a good education. I was living on 116 Central Park South—and in the penthouse. My friends were many. But my life was unhappy and sick. I had suffered twenty years with hay fever, fifteen years with ulcers and a half dozen perforated ulcers, enlarged liver and kidney stones. About twice a year I'd get jaundiced. I developed migraine headaches. Then heart trouble. And fear, anxiety and frustration all my life.

After my coronary I was told I might drop dead any minute. "Don't climb a stair unless you absolutely have to," I was warned.

That was in 1952. I was forty-three years old.

I was desperate.

This fear of dying scared me more than I've ever been scared in my life. It caused me to conclude with determination, "Either I get the answers, or I'll take me off this earth. No heart attack will do it!"

And I had a nice easy way to do it, too—morphine that the doctors had allowed me for my kidney stone attacks.

That determination to get the answers was the thing that gave me full realization of what life and happiness are.

After a few days of fear of dying, I resolved that there was nothing I could do brooding about it.

I started thinking of a way out. I sat alone in my apartment and just thinking, thinking, thinking.

I had a problem and had to get the answer. So I sat me down and said, "Lester, you were considered smart. You were an honor student in high school. You won a scholarship when only three scholarships to Rutgers University were awarded through competitive, statewide examinations. You were an honor student in college." But for all of that, I was dumb! dumb! dumb! I did not know how to get the very elementary thing in life—how to be happy!

Well, what do I do?

All of my past knowledge was useless. So I decided to drop it all and start from scratch.

Okay. Well, what am I? What is this world? What is my relationship to it?

I began reviewing the little happiness I had known and it was always related to a woman.

"Oh, being loved by a woman is what happiness is!" Then I thought, "Well, here I am. I've had and still have lovely women wanting me. But I am still miserable!"

I thought, "Then it's not being loved!" I began reviewing it again and I discovered that when I was loving them—then, I was happy.

Conclusion: my happiness equates to my capacity to love.

Then I went through a very keen process of trying to love others. I would review my past behavior. Where I thought I had been loving, I saw I wanted to be loved. For instance, when I saw that I had been nice to a girl only because I wanted something from her, I would say, "You son-of-a-gun, Lester. Correct that!" Then I would love her for what she was, not for what I wanted from her. I kept on correcting this until I could find no more to correct.

The next big awareness that came to me was what intelligence is. I got a picture of a single overall intelligence that each one of us is blindly using, available to us to the degree we do not cut off. I also discovered that I am responsible for everything that happens to me. Then I discovered that every thought materializes, sooner or later. Thereafter I took responsibility for everything that was happening to me. Looking for it, the initiating thought would come up in mind, and it being conscious, I would then be able to drop it.

I was letting go and undoing the hell I had created. By squaring all with love, trying to love rather than trying to be loved, and by taking responsibility for all that was happening to me; finding my subconscious thought and correcting it, I became freer and freer, happier and happier.

The picture of intelligence that I received I think is interesting. I suddenly got a picture of the amusement park entertainment consisting of bump-cars that are made difficult to steer so that the drivers continually bump into each other.

They were all getting their electrical energy from the wire screen above, through a pole coming down to every car. The power above was symbolic of the overall intelligence and energy of the universe coming down the pole to me and everyone else, which we were all using and bumping into each other, instead of driving along together in harmony.

We use this intelligence in life and we just bump! bump! bump! That was the first picture I got of life and intelligence.

We all have a direct line to that infinite intelligence up there and we are using it blindly, wrongly, and against each other.

For the first two months I was getting answers to, "What is happiness, intelligence and love?" As the answers came, I was gradually being unburdened of my miseries and tensions.

The very first insight was on love, seeing that my happiness was determined by my capacity to love. That was a tremendous insight. It began to free me. Any bit of freedom when you're plagued feels so good. I knew that I was in the right direction. I had gotten hold of a link of a chain and was determined not to let go until I had the entire chain.

Then I saw that my sum-total thinking was responsible for everything happening to me, and that gave me more freedom. I could control my life by undoing the compulsive behavior, all of which had been determined in the past, and was now subconscious.

The third phase was discovering and recognizing who and what I really am. I began to see that we are infinite beings with no limitations; that all limitations were only concepts in our minds, learned in the past, and being held on to.

When we see what we really are, we can see that we are not that limited being that we had thought we were, and we can then easily drop the limitations.

Working on those three things, I became freer and freer. My heart became lighter. I was happier, more at peace. My mind got quieter. Then my curiosity took me all the way. I said, "If this is so good, I must find just how good it can get. I'll go the limit."

I'd had a life mostly of misery. So when this wonderful thing of happiness began coming in, I wanted all of it. I doggedly kept at it.

And then all of a sudden powers fell in on me. I could know anything anywhere.

I saw there were people just like us on endless numbers of planets.

Then I took a look across the country to Los Angeles. I called up this friend and said, "In the living room there are three persons," and so on. I started telling him what was going on. Dead air! Suddenly I realized I had frightened him. I had to cut the conversation short.

I was amazed at the very pleasant sensation of watching divine laws in operation. The fascination was not the powers themselves, but the watching and witnessing of the divine laws operating. I really didn't feel like the doer.

I knew these things were not to be latched on to. I knew that if I got interested in them, I'd stop progressing.

I had seen by this time that this world is a mentation—a dream. So to get interested in the dream again through interest in powers would trap me back into what I was wanting to get out of.

Toward the end of my period of seeking, I one day saw that, my gosh! This whole thing is like a dream in my mind, just like a night dream! And it's a dream that never really was—any more than a dream you had last night was. Was it a real thing, that dream you had last night? No. It was only in your mind. But of course until one awakens out of this everyday waking state, it seems real to one.

The new reality was that I am, and that's all there is! That my beingness is the changeless essence of the universe, of course, I was punch-drunk, slap-happy, and in a state of euphoria.

In this state the whole world looks perfect. Looking at my body, I also saw this body as part of that perfection. This instantly corrected all my ailments.

Several times on the way up I'd get a realization that would so supercharge my body, I'd have to walk for miles and miles at a good pace.

Some of those realizations are really more than a body can take. You can't sit still. Many a time I was forced to walk off the new, intense energy.

I was undoing the subconscious hang-ups, tendencies, predispositions, realizing more and more that I am free, that freedom is my basic nature. I was getting freer and freer and I automatically went into a state where, having undone enough of the mental limitations, the real Self of me began presenting itself to me.

I saw that the real "I" of me was only beingness, was only existence, and that my beingness was exactly the beingness of the universe. And when I saw that, I identified with every being in this universe; I identified with every atom in it. And when you do that you lose all sense of being a separate individual, an ego.

When I saw that, that I AM the Amness of this universe, I then saw the whole world as just an image in my imagination, like a dream.

I imaged or dreamt that I was a body. And I'm dreaming right now that I'm this body.

In reality, the only thing that is, is Isness. That's the real, changeless substance behind everything.

And you are that, too.

When I started, I couldn't have been much lower. I was plagued with all these ailments accumulated over the years topped with a coronary, and with deep depths of depression and intense misery.

Three months later I was at the other extreme; I was so happy I had a smile on my face that I could not take off. I felt a euphoria and lightness that is really indescribable.

Everything of life itself was open to me—the total understanding of it. It is simply that we are infinite beings, over which we have superimposed concepts of limitation. And we are smarting under these limitations that we accept for ourselves as though they are real, because they are opposed to our basic nature of total freedom. However, they are just mentations, mental concepts.

Life before and after was at two different extremes. At first it was just extreme depression and sickness. After, it was a happiness and serenity that's indescribable.

Life itself became so beautiful and so harmonious that all day every day everything would fall perfectly into line. As I would drive through New York City, I would rarely hit a red light.

When I would go to park my car, people, sometimes two or three people, would stop and even go into the street to help direct me into a parking space. There were times when taxicab drivers would see me looking for a parking space and would give up their space so I could go into it. And after they did they couldn't understand why they did it. Here they were out, double-parked!

Even policemen who were parked would move out and give me their parking place. And, again, after they did it, they couldn't understand why they gave up their place to me. But I knew they felt good in doing what they had done. And I was thankful all the time.

But there wasn't anything I did in those days that didn't seem to affect everyone around me. My vibration made them feel good. It made them feel giving. It made them more loving. And so they would try to help me.

If I went into a store, the salesman would happily go out of his way to help me. Or if I would order something in a restaurant and after change my mind, the waitress would bring just what I wanted even though I didn't tell her. Actually everyone moves to serve you as you just float around.

When you are in tune and you have a thought, every atom in the universe moves to fulfill your thought. And this is true.

Being in harmony is such a delightful, delectable state, not because things are coming your way, but because of the feeling of God-in-operation. It's a tremendous feeling, you just can't imagine how great it is. It is such a delight when you're in tune, in harmony—you see God everywhere! You're watching God in operation. And that is what you enjoy, rather than the thing, the incident, the happening. His operation is the ultimate.

When we get in tune, our capacity to love is so extreme that we love everyone with an extreme intensity which makes living the most delightful it could ever be.

# A.C.

## Life
## After
## Consciousness

## *LOVE BEARS ALL THINGS*

## *LOVE BELIEVES ALL THINGS*

I got the feeling that I wanted everyone, the rest of me, to know what I had discovered. That was the first thing that hit me. But how could I do it?

I thought I could be most effective in getting this knowledge to children through the educational system, especially to children from the first grade on.

It came to me that there would be entire villages in Long Island available because of non-payment of FHA mortgaged towns.

Were I in the real estate business, I'd be in a position to step in. I decided to go into it. However, after I had gotten into it, one day while contemplating, it came to me that I had no right to interfere in the relationship of children and their parents who wanted them to get the conventional training. It would be interfering with the karma of a child and the parent. So I had to let go of that plan.

Karma is the law of compensation. Everything you give out comes back to you. I had no right to interfere in what was going to be the children's way of life, because their life was going to be in accordance with choices they had made.

I realized that the only thing I should do was to present my discovery to those who wanted to it.

And that I knew I was going to do.

The second thing that hit me was that I must prove everything, and being a scientist, that was natural. If I proved everything I could be more effective when I would talk about it.

So I went through a process of proving all this new knowledge that came to me. I began imaging things that I wanted, small things, and they came very quickly.

Then I realized that the only things that stopped me from getting something big, was that I just didn't dare to think big. So I asked myself, "What's the biggest thing I can think of in the way of things?" And I said, "Gee! A Cadillac, with a specially built body." I pictured a Cadillac with a specially built body, and I saw myself handling it and riding in it, and it was mine. Then I let go of the picture because I was so sure I had it.

In about two weeks, an acquaintance came to me and said, "Lester, I just bought you the most beautiful Cadillac," and he described it. It was the color I had in mind, everything just as I had seen it. He said, "A friend of mine bought it, got a specially built body, but he doesn't want it, and I got it for only $4,000."

When he said that, I looked at him. I didn't have the money.

"Oh, don't worry about the money," he said, "I'll pay for it."

I said to him, "Well, will you give me until tomorrow to give you my answer?"

He quizzically looked at me. Who takes a day to give an answer to a thing like that? But he said, "Yes, sure."

I thought it over. I had just gotten rid of my old car. In New York City, it was a nuisance. Also, I didn't like the idea of being ostentatious with a Cadillac. I felt a unity with people. Most people didn't have Cadillacs and I did not want to be in a position that would make them envious. I also thought, "Well, if I did it now, I can do it any time."

So when tomorrow came, I refused the car. It was quite a surprise and almost a shock to my friend.

And likewise, I proved out every other law that I realized.

I knew from the very beginning that I would have to come back in to the world. But I was so far out, I couldn't at that time.

Everybody's mind was a wide open book. I would say to a person, if you would do this, your problem would resolve. I could zero in on what they needed and I'd give it to them in one sentence. But it was too far away from them. It was of little effect.

Sometimes I would answer questions without being asked, or someone would ask me a question and my answer would be something entirely unrelated to the question. I was answering what people really wanted to know rather than the voiced question.

Then I became aware that there were groups who were studying this subject—metaphysics. What I knew couldn't be put into words—yet there were groups talking about it! I decided that I should meet the people who were talking about these things. And I was led into it.

I read all the major schools of metaphysics to acquire their language to speak to all people, only to discover that the very best language was the most simple and to-the-point: everyday English.

I used to go often to Steinway Hall in New York, attending various metaphysical lectures, and I met people there that I helped in small ways. But just a few individuals, that's all. I'm not a mass teacher.

To my family the change in me was puzzling.

My sister Doris phoned to invite me to supper. Before she could ask me, I said, "Okay, Doris, I'll be there for supper. I'll see you in fifteen minutes," and I hung up. Then I realized she hadn't even asked me!

I would visit my brother-in-law Nat, and my sister, and Nat would say, "Lester, you're an engineer. Fix my radio."

I'd look at it and say, "Nat, it's just that loose tube." I'd tighten it in its socket and the set would work.

Well, after I did this six or eight times, Nat caught on and said, "Hey, Lester. There's something strange about this. Every time my radio or hi-fi goes bad, it's always just a loose tube, and you tighten it and it starts playing. How come?"

I said, "It just happens to be a loose tube, Nat." I knew he wouldn't believe me if I told him. He couldn't accept the unusual.

I just saw the radio as perfect and only adjusted the tube to make it understandable to him.

After my realization, I wanted to prove to others that you can have anything you want. I even became a millionaire.

I started a real estate business. My thinking was, "How many buildings can I buy in Manhattan if I have no money invested in each one?" That's what I had at the time—no money!

With no cash invested in each building, I saw that I could buy the entire island of Manhattan! I proceeded with that idea.

The first buildings I bought were two ten-family houses, contiguous as one unit. The price I got it for was so good, that when the bank appraised it, the mortgage offered was more than the purchase price by a thousand dollars.

So now I had two buildings and an additional thousand dollars. Next, I put five hundred dollars down as deposit on a contract for eighteen one-family houses in a row on East 79th Street. Within three weeks I sold the contract for a twenty thousand dollar profit.

In about two years' time, I owned twenty-three apartment houses with twenty to forty units per house. They were all bought with no cash by buying them on first and second mortgages and, if and when necessary, with an additional personal loan from my lawyer. The income from the buildings had to be enough to make all payments, including amortization of all mortgages, and yet show a profit.

The properties were building up a beautiful equity.

Every deal that I was in had to be good for everyone involved. That was one secret of my success.

I would go to the banks and ask if they had any real estate for sale. I discovered there were many estates that were being liquidated. When they wanted to liquidate older apartments, and older apartments would not sell quickly and so they would sell them for roughly one-half market price. I would immediately buy them without even looking at them. I quickly sold them for three-quarter market price.

Things were going along beautifully. And I spent most of the time contemplating, working only four hours a day, if that much.

As I was deep in contemplation one day, I was hit with this: "Now walk out of here with just the shirt on your back as Jesus did. Just walk out with nothing but that which you can carry."

I immediately stood up and walked to the door. I said, "Wait a minute, Lester. There are first mortgages, second mortgages and personal loans on these buildings. See to it that these people are taken care of first."

That decision was a mistake. I should have given it to God and everyone would have been taken care of.

Well, after I got that inner direction, I unloaded the real estate at giveaway prices, that is, all except five buildings that I could not sell because they were lemons. I had bought them because I was told that they were going to be condemned in a few months by the city for a new housing project, and therefore would be profitable.

I turned those buildings over to a broker to take care of, bought a new Chrysler car, and left for the West.

I wanted an isolated spot somewhere, and found this acreage I'm now on in Sedona, Arizona, 160 acres at the end of the road, naturally isolated away from everything. A perfect place for a retreat!

I told the broker I'd take it, even though I had no money for the deposit. In a day or two, a check came in the mail to tie it up.

I hadn't known the check was coming. It was a small check from the real estate in New York. With it I put a down payment on this property. Shortly after, I got notice that the city wanted those five buildings. With the money from them, I was able to close the deal and pay cash for the land.

Since 1958 when I left New York, I've been supported by letting go and letting God do it.

You see, another thing that came to me when I got that direction to walk out of my New York apartment with only the shirt on my back. It was that accumulation is non-conviction. If I am taken care of, I have no need to accumulate. Do birds and animals have need to accumulate? If God will take care of them, He certainly will take care of me.

If you have full confidence you're going to be taken care of, you don't have any thought of future security. The only security there really is, is to be able to produce at will.

From that day on, everything that I needed came to me as I needed it. And it's still that way.

## *LOVE FLOURISHES IN LOVE*

When I came to Sedona, Arizona in 1958 I had no plans. I parked my body here and remained in the state of ecstasy for approximately two years. I was alone during this time, but I was impelled from within to go out on occasion.

I went to New York to speak to small groups. Notes were taken and from them was published "The Ultimate Truth Book."

From that, other groups formed spontaneously. I would talk to them for a few sessions, leave and then return in a half a year or so. They'd gather again, the same people with additional people, and again I'd hold sessions with them. The time lapse was to allow them to assimilate.

However, I quit doing this a year ago.

I really never saw myself as a teacher and I have no wish to start anything like a new movement. People were pulling on me and I was giving because they were pulling. In the process they starting taping these sessions in 1964. Because of those tapes, we now have the printed series of "Sessions with Lester." That can be found in The Ultimate Truth Book.

My coming back into the world had made me see things differently. When I originally talked to groups I never saw any opposition. It was God talking to God.

But now, I see much opposition coming at me from people. I never saw it originally. Now, I see it as my imposing when they are opposing what I'm telling them.

I feel I have no right to impose. Now I can present what I have to say in black and white and they can read it or not, as they choose. I no longer feel the need to go out anymore.

I see that most people don't want the truth. What they want is to make the world a better world. That's fine and I'm happy for them to have a better world. They're welcome to use the data that comes through me for that purpose. It is a step forward.

Most of the people seeking, I'd say ninety-five percent of them, are only seeking a good life. They're not seeking the ultimate. When they get to that place where they can make life nice and easy and comfortable, they stop their growth.

They go so high and life gets so easy—and then they level off. But what happens is that they can't remain happy. They'll never be satisfied until they go all the way. So there they are stuck. I can point out a group in Los Angeles that I had worked closely with. Their businesses became good. The couples got along exceptionally well. Life became a ball. But now, four years later they feel awful. Business is not good as it used to be. They get headaches and they're very frustrated. They really are miserable.

There is no standing still. If one is not going forward, he is going backward. If he is going in the direction of the world, he is in the opposite direction of freedom from limitation, as the world is of limitation.

Eventually, though, everyone makes it. That's what we're all being driven toward when we're looking for happiness in the world. We're really looking for the highest and most felicitous state there is. In the world we call it happiness. But happiness isn't there, and sometime, sooner or later, we learn that and then take the right direction.

All of my teachings are now in print and in a course called "The Abundance Course" (See the back of this book for more information). But the ones who really want what I can give are few. To quote, "Of a thousand, one seeks Me. Of a thousand who seek Me, one finds Me."

We are in a world period that is so ignorant of truth. We are so blinded that we are seeking the way of the spirit via materiality. We are seeking to make the material an ideal materiality, more cars, more machines, more power, and more money.

Our God today is the dollar. This country worships the dollar more than anything else. By worship, I mean we're devoted to it. You think businessmen are not devoted to money? They eat, breathe and sleep it. They really worship, but worship money. And because of it, they're unhappy, there is no peace or serenity for them.

When I first arrived in Arizona I just sat for two years in isolation. I withdrew into that beautiful high state. The only thing similar to it in your experience would be deep sleep with no dream, where you feel so good when you wake up, and you remember it.

I was in that state, but aware. That state is awareness itself. When you're in that state, any particular thing that's necessary to become conscious of, you do.

It was definitely a withdrawal from the world. Yet, all the time, I held on to my commitments that I'm now going through.

I again spoke to small groups, especially in Los Angeles and New York after two years. In 1962 I went to Phoenix and that brought me more into contact with people. From 1965 to 1970 I was pretty active, most of the time in Los Angeles, as follows.

I bumped into an unusual scientist. His idea was to do away with poverty world-wide, by tapping the energy of the atom.

I managed a $300,000 project for him. We worked to produce aluminum metal that would have a higher thermal conductivity than silver. Silver has the highest of any known metal. This would lead to higher electrical conductivity that would lead to tapping the energy in the atom.

While in L.A. I became active in teaching groups.

My purpose was to come back more so into the world. Coming back to the world is to me, simply behaving as though the world is miserable and difficult as most people see it.

Once you realize how effortless the highest way of life is, it takes tremendous effort to assume the opposite.

# Fourth

## Wisdom of the "Why's"

## *LOVE IS CONTAGIOUS*

In the beginning after my realizations, I was involved in individual healings. One thing would be healed and after that there would be another. Then it came to me that it would be far better to teach people to heal themselves.

Spiritual healing is the best; it's instantaneous. If you cannot do it spiritually, do it mentally. That's from instantaneous to quick. However, if you cannot use these two, then see a doctor. To each his own.

Spiritual healing is done by knowing the perfection that is. It causes you to let go of the imperfection by seeing only the perfection.

Mental healing is taking your mind off the sickness, and thinking of or visualizing your body as healthy. It is impossible to be sick without holding the picture of it in your mind!

I was involved with healing only for a short while, from 1952 to 1956 and only on an individual scale. People who went along with it did have instantaneous healings, even over the telephone.

Once a girl phoned me an said, "I've been to the doctor and he said I've got a ruptured diaphragm. He wants to operate. What should I do?"

I saw her as whole and perfect and said, "Just look at it as being all perfect. You're all okay."

And she said, "Yeah! That's right!" I felt her acceptance of the perfection.

I then told her, "All right, now go back to the doctor for a check up." She did and she no longer had it. The doctor was astonished.

I didn't attract any attention to myself with these healings. I was always in the background. You do not feel yourself as the healer; you just get yourself out of the way. You let go and let God. And, as you do this, the healing happens.

Jesus said that it was the Father who worketh through Him. A mass teacher has to go out and talk to the masses. But he's not ostentatious about it. He feels that it is God talking to God.

Jesus said that unless ye see signs, ye believe not. So He gave people signs to help them believe. All these healings are done to help someone get some spiritual revelation. Healing for the sake of healing is not really done. It has to be more than that.

In my growth I have always held in the back of my mind, that I only know that which I can do. If I say I can do something, I don't know it unless I do it. This kept me from fooling me.

However there is a paradox, here. If I Lester, try to perform a miracle, I cannot. If I succeed in getting Lester out of the way by letting go and letting God, then it happens.

There must be no sense of doership here.

Radical reliance on God is what does it.

If someone tries to perform a miracle and it doesn't work for him, then his knowledge is not complete. You must have the understanding. You must get your little self out of the way. You must let go and let God, and it happens immediately. But you do not think of trying it out or testing it. You know it is and you just let it be.

People ask me, "Lester, can you do miracles?"

I say, "No, I can't." That's the truth. Yet there isn't anything I have not experienced by getting me, Lester, out of the way. By letting go of the sense of egoity, anything and everything can happen.

As Jesus said, "In my Father's house are many mansions." After people drop the body they go into a world similar to this where they meet old friends. The main difference is that everything there is immediate. Whatever you think comes into being right away. So much easier a life than this.

It's heavenly, compared to this. But because of its being so easy, there's little incentive to grow. Here, the opportunity for growth is the greatest.

If you die with an intense desire to stay with something here, you stay with it. Big executives come back to sit in their chairs, and they're furious because there's another guy in there, and they can't get him out. People who want something here hang on, and they're the ghosts.

Some of them are able to make a little noise like a rap on the wall, or to move blankets and small things like that. But that's as far as they can go. They can't do anything to us, though some people are frightened of them.

There is nothing in the universe that can harm us but our acceptance of the thoughts that we can be harmed.

I notice from B.C. experience that when I had confidence, it transferred over to others. I can explain it now. Anything we have an absolute conviction of is, or very quickly becomes so. I was so confident I was going to get a loan from the bank! I knew it without a doubt, and that caused the banker to lean in my direction and give me a $10,000 loan without security.

Everyone reads everyone else's mind, unconsciously. When two people meet, I smile sometimes at how they react to each other, unconsciously reading each other. I'm aware of it. We all read each other.

I was against all those things in the days before realization. I'd try to reason them out, unsuccessfully, then I'd throw them out as nonsense.

I used to work seven days a week, twelve to fourteen hours a day, driven by inner anxieties. I was relieved from them by keeping myself occupied all the time. That was the main reason I worked so hard. I excused it by saying I was always starting businesses with no money, so I had to work hard. But I didn't. It was just escape.

This point should be brought out: I lived life the way a person should live it, in that I tried to be good, make money, be the best in my profession. I tried to do all the things everyone is trying to do. I was after the goals that were accepted by society—success, wealth, being known, or renowned.

And I tried to do it within the rules. But I kept going down, down, down in physical and mental health, until I came to the near-end with the coronary.

No matter how you strive the way you're supposed to, in accordance with the rules of society, even achieving its goals, you do not get what you want.

You wind up behind the eight ball. The world is actually set up that way. You can't win in the world.

The world is set up that way, hellish, so that we will someday transcend it and go back to being anything but a limited physical body, which is the least thing we could ever be.

I was extremely suppressed, unable to express my feelings. I became suppressed because, not understanding the world and wanting acceptance, I would suppress all my own feelings in order to have the approval of others. I did this from the earliest of years, and it caused me to be quite neurotic.

Carrying out the directions that the world thought right, wanting to do what they wanted, I suppressed my own feelings.

I could never understand the values of the world. I was never really interested in money. I never enjoyed it, because I was forcing myself to make money. I never liked competition. I felt it wasn't right. And even though I was an excellent handball player and tennis player—good enough to play with the champions—I could beat them out of competition, but I could never win in competition. So I could never be on the teams.

Competition didn't feel right. It was oppositional. It wasn't right for one to win over the other. Games of sport should be played just for the fun of it, the skill, the exercise, not to win.

During all the time of my seeking, sleep got less and less until it disappeared entirely. We need sleep for one reason only—to escape from this world we think is so real. We want it so much, but it's so heavy to us that we have to cut out from it on the average of eight hours a day.

When you're in tune and in harmony, you never get tired. Fatigue is only due to mental conflict. When all mental conflict is gone, you never, ever tire. All the energy in the universe is available to you when you're in tune. Should you want to use it, it's there for your use.

In the days that I didn't sleep, I had far more energy than at the time I did sleep. Wanting to be like other people, I started to sleep again. At first I tried it for an hour, then two hours, and finally up to six hours. Now I keep it that way, although it still is irregular.

I can sleep one hour or six. It's all the same to me now.

Before my realization, I believed the doctors and nutritionists who said I couldn't get too much protein. In the morning I'd have, with my eggs, a big ham steak or a rasher of bacon. At noon and at the evening meal, I'd always have meat.

When I got my realization, I saw that our animal family was related to us. I looked upon them as pets. Can a man eat his pets?

If a hunger pang turns on, I turn it off, and then it's gone.

So I never suffer from hunger.

This can be accomplished by anyone with practice. Do not eat when you're hungry, and eat when you're not hungry. You can still have three meals a day that way. It's just a method of mastering the body. You go into control instead of the stomach controlling you.

The happiest moments in my life before realization in 1952 were falling in love with beautiful girls. It was the same thing again and again. I'd fall madly in love, we'd eventually break apart, and I'd have the insides ripped out of me.

The first time I broke up was with Annette, the girl of high school and college days. It took me about five years to completely get over that. It hit me so hard, I used all my energies fighting it. I was in a constant gloom for a long time because of it.

Then I met Virginia and I fell in love with her. And then we broke up. This time, it took only three years to get over it.

Being in love was of more interest to me than anything else in life. My problem was that I was so unfree I just could not bear more of the non-freedom that I felt marriage would give me. And because I would not marry, the girls would leave me.

I didn't want to go through those agonies any more, so I had to do something about it. I knew the girls would leave me if I didn't marry them, so I evolved a system to prevent the extreme misery of parting.

When a love affair reached its height, and I could see it starting to go downhill, I would begin to get ready for the break.

But having suffered, I didn't want these girls to suffer the way I had. So I would have them throw me over.

I discovered that if a man chased a girl, she ran. If he ran away from her, she ran toward him. So, with words, I would start fencing them in with love. I'd say, "Honey, where have you been? You should have been here sooner. I need you around. Don't do that again." They'd get tight and uncomfortable. It was all fencing in, and I knew how to work it beautifully.

This was all head work. I just learned by watching what made people move. I really didn't understand it psychologically.

The total effect on me of my love affairs was misery!

But those blows of love, passion, and then heartbreak are really good. Were it not for the blows, we'd be forever sunk in this delusion, which is bits of pleasure and long periods of pain. That's the pattern in the world—for each ounce of pleasure we pay with pounds and pounds of pain. The pain is so great, most people get accustomed to it and don't even see the extent of it.

My first clue that a love relationship was starting to go downhill came when the girl first started hinting, then talking, and finally nagging, about marriage. When the nagging started, it was nearing the end. By that time, I would have another girl set, so that I wouldn't suffer the acute pain that formerly I had suffered.

There was nothing worse than that suffering. You can't turn it off. You can't put any salve on it, except the one salve I discovered—getting another girl!

In most love relationships, that which one wants from the other is mostly ego approval. That is why the majority of people are not happily married. They're picking at each other most of the time, wanting ego approval. That makes for a bad marriage.

What makes a successful marriage? Two things—having interests in common and friendship.

I was sitting in the 23rd Street Cafeteria in New York City with two friends. This was about 1945. We were sitting around the table having pie and coffee and Joe remarked, "Gee, I never have any sex."

And I said, "Joe, what about last weekend with so-and-so?"

And Joe said, "Oh, that doesn't count."

"And what about so-and-so the weekend before that?"

"Oh, that doesn't count."

"And what about so-and-so the weekend before that?"

"Oh, that doesn't count."

Then Fred chimed in, "Gee, I never have any sex either."

I said, "Fred, what about so-and-so last weekend?"

"Oh, that doesn't count."

"And what about so-and-so the weekend before that?"

"Oh, that doesn't count."

And then I got a tremendous realization. I saw that I, too, felt the same way: that I never have any sex! And I said, "Are we insane? What is this?" And I saw that what we wanted was not sex, but love. And not getting the love we were saying, "We're not having any sex."

I let go of the feeling that I never-have-sex after that, but it didn't help much. I still felt that I couldn't get love. I still felt that I didn't have love.

I think this is the reason why many people today are indulging in so much sex: they are identifying it with love, and not finding love through it they go in for more and more sex all the time.

You don't get free by fighting the world. You get free from within.

When Nancy Sinatra was asked on a talk show what she thought of the women's liberation movement, she said she couldn't understand it. She said, "Freedom is a personal thing. I don't feel that I have to fight for freedom."

She implied that she already felt she had that freedom.

The whole movement made no sense to her. And she had the right idea, that freedom is a state you achieve personally.

Women are acting like second-class citizens in our society—so much so, that many of them accept it and don't even see it!

The reason why women are in a secondary position is that they think of themselves as secondary. If they would correct their own thinking and actually think of themselves as equal to men in everything, they would be. Then the "women's lib" movement would be in every woman and there would be no need for the movement.

The Constitution of the U.S. has always given equal rights to all citizens—women included.

Yet, how many Presidents have been women? How many members of Congress are women? How many executives of corporations are women?

Most of the great masters we know have been men. Women who are masters do not have the acceptance that the world gives men, and therefore tend to remain out of sight.

The nature of man is reason; the nature of woman is feeling. Feeling is closer to the Self than reason. Therefore, women are closer to the Self in that they operate on feeling.

It reminds me of one businessman who never would make an important decision until he brought his client home for his wife's approval. He had learned from experience that her feeling or intuition was always right. He said he couldn't explain it, but he knew that it was so.

You see, there are two different natures, and this is why, sometimes, we have a difficult time understanding one another.

In some of the groups I've worked with, the men were always questioning. And they were brilliant. The women hardly ever said anything—but they moved beyond men! The women felt it, they experienced it. Women work by feeling; men by reasoning.

Women have the advantage.

It came to me why some men and women are homosexuals. As we go through our many, many lives, we change sex at certain times. For instance, if I had been a woman in my last lifetime, and this time I took on a male body, I'd have a certain amount of natural attraction for women because of my male body, but I'd have more of my feminine feelings carried over from my last lifetime. The more lifetimes I continue in a male body, the more masculine become my feelings, and the less homosexual I would be.

You find homosexuality among all peoples. It's natural. We change sex to get more experiences.

It is good that homosexuality is more accepted today. Until recently it was criminal to be that way. That was cruel.

I saw, too, that infants are not mental nothingnesses. If you'll remember back to the days you were an infant, even to the day you were born, you'll see that you knew who your mother was, who your father was, and even who the doctor was. You knew all these things, even though you couldn't talk. You knew what was going on.

Your only interests were to satisfy your needs. If Momma didn't give you milk, you cried, and Momma gave it to you.

My oldest sister spoke at the age of six months. But I didn't talk until I was three. This caused everyone to worry about me. They thought I was stupid. But I didn't need to talk. I got everything I wanted by pointing and making a sound. I used to wonder why they were worried about me.

Not needing to talk, I didn't until I was three—but I'm making up for it now!

After my realization, I went back in memory and relieved my infancy. What every infant wants, is his needs satisfied. If they are, he's happy; if they're not, he uses the only language he knows—crying!

A child should never be left to cry. It is not lung exercise. It's cruel to let a child cry without finding out what he wants and taking care of it. This taking care of the needs of children would alleviate much of their insecurity in adulthood.

Education today is a total miseducation.

You take an infinite being and you try to jam rote stuff into him, stifling his capacity to evolve and be creative. You're also stifling his evolution.

Do you have to teach a flower how to grow beautiful? We should have the same attitude toward a child. We should allow the child to evolve naturally, to express his inner abilities.

When you look at it that way, you can see how confining our educational system is.

Take the colleges. They tell you you must learn to think for yourself. But if you think differently from the professors, you flunk.

In my first term in college, I was told, "Now that I'm in college, I should think for myself." So I started doing it. The first two marking periods I flunked all the subjects where I had to think for myself.

I really struggled with it, until finally I asked one of the professors if he would allow me to see the exam papers of the others who got good marks.

I read them and discovered that they were giving him back exactly what he was telling us.

Then I saw the whole picture: if I thought the way he thought, I was smart; if I didn't, I was dumb, even though he told me to think for myself.

So it's not true that they want you to think for yourself; they want you to think the way they think.

After that, it was easy. I kept excellent notes and made sure I always gave back the prof his ideas. With the least amount of studying, I got the best marks.

All drugs are poisons. Poisons tend to push you out of your body and give you a feeling of detachment from its heaviness. By letting go of the attachment to the body, you expand your consciousness beyond the body consciousness.

The harm of smoking marijuana or taking any drug is that you give it the credit for doing something that you can and should do without it. Being high is our natural state, and must be gotten by our own doingness. The more we use marijuana or other drugs, the more we depend on them to feel high. Therefore the less capable we become of being high on our own.

Also, when we do it on our own horsepower rather than with drugs, we can go way beyond the limits of the highness that the drugs allow, and experience the way beyond the most fantastic of our imaginings. You see, there is actually no limit to how high we can go on our own, without drugs.

One thing, however: Marijuana could be an eye-opener in that it may give you a preview of something you might never have had without it. But I don't advocate taking drugs. You can get the same preview with more intensity by just getting your mind quiet enough.

Cancer, close to Leo, is my astrological sign. Astrological data has been accumulated by compilation of the lives of many, many known people. Therefore, it fits many people.

But my opinion is that, as much as those planets out there influence me, how much influence does this planet earth have on me? Earth is not thrown into consideration of the planets when astrologers develop your charts. Yet, its influence is greater than all the other planets put together.

Also, who is smarter? Clods of soil out there in space, or my intelligence? The planets are matter. Should they determine my intelligence? I say, no! This is my attitude towards astrology. When matter like planets determines us, we should turn it around and determine for the planets. I'm not going to subject myself to a distant clod of dirt guiding and influencing me.

Although intelligence is defined as the ability to resolve new problems, I define it as the ability to be happy. Man wants happiness more than anything else. Should not his intelligence be judged by his ability to get what he most wants?

You use your car to take you around, but you don't say, "I am the car." Likewise, your body is a carcass, or better, a "car-case." You're using it as a vehicle now. If you say, "I am the body," it's the same as you driving your car and saying, "I am the car."

## *LOVE IS THE MEANS AND THE END*

The word "atom," by definition, means the smallest indivisible particle. Up until 1952, having been trained in physics, I carefully followed the latest findings of the atom and atomic theory. The atom, which originally was supposed to have been the basic building block of the universe, already had more than thirty particles in it. I saw that it could no more be accepted as the indivisible building block.

I saw that our total knowledge of all natural phenomena added up to zero. We didn't know what gravity, magnetism, electricity, light or heat were.

Science progresses by trial and error, because science today doesn't understand natural phenomena. The reason for it is man's low understanding of the science of being. The world is on a destructive course because of that lack of understanding.

Today, we get our energy by destroying matter. If you keep destroying matter, by natural principle, it's going to destroy you. And that's what's happening in the world today. An eye for an eye, a tooth for a tooth—the law of compensation!

We've poisoned the atmosphere with our destruction of the fossil fuels, coal and oil. Now it's poisoning us.

We're poisoning the water. And we're poisoning the food. We can't go on doing this and survive.

We must go with nature rather than destroy it. We must learn that if we do not and continue our present direction, it will destroy us. This is already becoming obvious.

We can and we must. And the way is by the study of man and his beingness. The science that would correct all other sciences as it is basic to all their sciences.

Sooner or later we must understand the science of nature, understand the atom and then we'll use the atom in which is unlimited free energy.

If we would let go of our destructiveness and hate, the mind would be cleared so that we could see the simplicity of nature and natural law. It is not complicated as our physicists try to make it.

Natural, infinite power is right there in front of our eyes and we can't see it. Nature is here to serve us. We're not here to fight it, smash it, or crash it. But everything we do, we do the hard way. Our basic research instrument, the cyclotron, smashes atoms.

That's because the major science, that is the basic science of all sciences, the science of being, man has little or no interest in. The science of being would explain and make all the other sciences known.

If we were in tune with nature, in tune with ourselves, loving rather than hating, nature would be allowed to fulfill and serve us with a bounty that would make everyone not only affluent, but also extremely happy.

We have theories that we keep changing. Every physicist is aware of this. If they were correct they would need no change. The atom was supposed to be the basic building-block that everything else is built out of. We know now that that theory is wrong. And yet, we hold on to it.

Gravity and magnetism we don't understand. We don't even know what electricity is, but we can use it. Through trial and error we've learned how. By crossing a magnetic field with a copper conductor, we get a current.

We've learned to produce electricity that way. Why it happens, we still don't know.

We don't understand gravity—nothing about it, and that's why we are so earthbound. When we discover what it is, we will freely and easily travel the universe.

Everything in nature goes two ways. If there's a plus, there's a minus; if there's a hot, there's a cold; and if there's gravity, there's anti-gravity. Only when we understand gravity will we have the key to anti-gravity. Only then, we can leave this planet and travel the universe. We will travel on the magnetic lines of the universe.

While man is of the destructive mind that he is now, nature keeps him bound to his planet. Otherwise he would go to other planets to conquer them. He would cause havoc and destroy the harmony of the universe.

So nature confines him here. When we get more understanding, more loving, and therefore our minds quieter, we'll begin to see the natural law. Then we'll see what gravity is, and how to leave this planet with ease.

We'll see how to get unlimited free energy from the atom in a non-destructive way.

We do know that the energy is there. We use it in our atomic bombs.

As I've said before, our research into the atom is by smashing it's cyclotrons. We learn by destruction, a very unfortunate approach.

We must reverse and learn by constructing. Then we'd get the correct answers. We should look at the universe out there, and learn how it is constructing itself and, in the process, the atom. In knowing how the atom is constructed is the secret to its unlimited power.

The atom of our physical universe is the photon particle. It's the smallest particle we are capable of measuring. As the light particle, it hits our retina and registers as light. That same particle is basically the force of gravity and magnetism, and the energy level of the atom.

But this is way-out physics and physicists will say that it is ridiculous.

Matter is nothing but energy standing at a point. Physicists know this. There is a certain amount of energy standing still in this coffee cup resting on this table. When the cup moves, it becomes energy. If I hit you with this cup, you'd know there was energy coming at you. It is really that simple.

From the highest point of view I saw that matter is frozen energy, and energy is nothing more than mind in motion. That all of it is just mentation! The whole universe is only a mentation. The whole thing is an image in our minds!

This I try to show by saying, park your mind, go to sleep. Then where is this world? Don't wake up, and it never is again!

Where is that world but in your mind? Put your mind away permanently and there never again is the world.

When you see your oneness, when you see your real Self, you see this entire universe as a dream in your mind, just as in night-dream.

You imagine all your dreams, the characters in them, the action going on, the relationship between characters. The same way you wake up out of a night-dream, some day you wake up out of this waking-state dream to the fact that you're dreaming the whole thing.

You'll say, "Oh, my gosh! It's nothing but a dream!" And you'll laugh and that's the end of your being an effect of the illusion. If you come back to it, you'll try to help the rest of you wake up.

My definition of real is: That which never changes is real. The reality is changeless. It is absolute—truth never changes. It is always true.

Let me give you an illustration that comes from the East: You're walking along the road at dusk and there's a rope on the ground. You imagine it to be a snake. Then you get all wrought up and involved in the fear of that snake and what it can do to you.

Now the snake represents the world. The rope represents the reality. The rope is harmless, emotionless and changeless.

But that snake is a terrible, dangerous thing.

The world is like that snake, an imagining, an illusion. All questions of the world are like questions about the snake. Will this snake attack me? How can I protect myself from the snake, and so forth and so on.

It's all about something that really isn't! The reality is the rope. The reality of the world is the beingness behind it.

When you get your realization, the world doesn't disappear, but your knowledge of it changes completely. Instead of the world being separate, out of your control, you discover that it only exists because of your beingness. You're image-ing the whole thing.

Then you see it as a dream, while before it seemed to be so real to you. That's the only difference before and after realization.

But as long as you think the rope is a snake, you're very involved with it.

I could give it to you another way, too.

The world is an illusion, just like an oasis on the desert. When you look over a desert, it sometimes looks as though there is water there. As long as you don't go over and check it, you'll always think it's water.

When you go to the spot, you discover there is no water there, only sand. The next time you look at it, you still see the illusion with this difference. Now you know it's an illusion.

When you know your real Self, you discover it's totally sufficient unto itself, that you have satiety, or everything you want. And you drop your thirst for the oasis.

## *LOVE SEEKS ITS OWN LIKENESS*

There is a natural way for each nature to achieve realization.

What's natural to you is the best way for you. That's why there are four major ways that embrace everyone's nature.

The four ways are the rational, which is the mental way; the scientific, which is the specific methodological way; the emotional, which is the love and devotional way; and the active way, which is rendering selfless service to mankind.

To uncover yourself it takes only wanting to and looking in the right direction.

When you look for the I-that-I-am, it has to be sought just behind the mind. The mind can never conceive of infinity because the mind itself is finite.

When your mind is quiet enough so that you'll see through the noise of the mind, then you'll see the real "I" that you are.

The more you work to quiet the mind, the more you succeed. You keep it up until complete success is there.

Mind is only creative. What we hold in mind comes into actual manifestation. The mind thinks in pictures. If I say the word "shoe," the mind pictures a shoe, and not the word.

The mind cannot picture the words "not" and "don't." Whatever you "don't," you're holding the picture of what you don't want, and therefore you're creating that which you don't want. When I say to myself, "Don't forget your watch, Lester," I forget my watch. If I say, "Don't spill the tea," the tea spills.

It's a weird thing to watch. The first thing I used to get me back with the world was negative words. At first I had no negative words in my vocabulary.

You'd be surprised how many negative words most people use. Check it. You'll see some interesting results.

Well, for me it was natural not to use them. So when I started learning how to come back into the world I had to latch on to "don'ts." It's an established habit for me now. It helps me stay with people.

But remember, the mind is only creative. If you "don't" something, you're holding in mind the picture of something you do not want, but will create. You see, "don't" is not a picture in the mind, but the thing you are "don'ting" is. If you say, "Don't fall," "fall" is the picture.

You can throw anything out of your mind that you really want to. Anything you resolve to do, you do.

We should think in positives. I say to people, "Give me the opposite of the negative you're thinking," and they can't do it. The difficulty is habit. But you can change a negative habit to a positive habit.

Just put in a positive thought with more power than the negative habitual thought. It'll overwhelm and knock out the negative thought. One powerful thought can knock out hundreds of negative subconscious thoughts at once.

What makes the difference in the power of a thought? The amount of resolve, determination, or willpower that you put behind the thought.

If you can pose and hold the question "What am I?" until what you really are presents itself, this is the fastest way to complete freedom. I have yet to meet the person who has done it. But if you'd stay around the clock with only "What am I?" rejecting all other thoughts, in a matter of a few weeks, you'd have it.

In any event, you should always have "What am I?" in the back of your mind regardless of what you're doing.

If you're not successful with that, then the next big step is to drop your ego sense. When there's no more ego, what's left over is the infinite you.

If taking on the ego all at once seems too much at first, then start by dropping the effects of the ego, your tendencies, predispositions, likes and dislikes. Everyone can drop tendencies and predispositions easily, if he really wants to.

Start with the small ones and go on to bigger ones as I've told you. The simple tendency to walk on the right side of the street can be changed to walking on the left. The tendency to sleep eight hours can be changed to sleeping six.

Habitual tendencies don't have to be cut out permanently—just for a time, to demonstrate who is the master.

The tendency to seek approval is a big one to deal with. Everyone's attention is taken up in seeking approval. Everyone is doing it, and it's such a waste of effort and time.

Let me say that when you seek, whether it's with the ultimate question, "What am I?" or by dropping the ego sense or tendencies, isolation is necessary. Get quiet.

Isolation helps you quiet the mind. However, isolation can be had even in the city, or wherever you are. I isolated at 116 West 59th Street in the heart of New York City.

It's possible to grow every day through all our different relationships and meetings. We're here for growth, not a test. This is not a proving ground, it's a learning ground, a schoolroom.

There are different grades of schoolrooms for different planets. This one is a postgraduate course. It is of the most difficult, and therefore affords the greatest growth. All of us who are here are advanced souls—advanced in that we have chosen an extremely difficult place of abode. We wanted a higher course, a tougher one, and we've got it!

The vast majority of people's concept of love is actually hate, more or less. "I need you, I must have you, I can't live without you, you're mine," is all non-love.

Love is letting the other one have what the other one wants. Not what I want. What we call love in this world is usually a sensual, selfish emotion—a deal—if you do what I want I love you, and if you don't do it, I don't love you.

Sex and love are often tied in as the same, and they're not. If you want to know what sex is, observe the animals. Sex is a means of procreation. If we were living normal sex lives, we'd use sex only for that purpose. Man superimposes love on sex.

Fortunately and unfortunately, sex brings us closest to God. It usually brings out the finest of our feelings. It is fortunate in that we begin to get a taste of our feelings of love, and unfortunate in that it pegs us there and prevents us from getting deeper and intenser feelings of love.

Unknown to most is that when our love is capable of being expressed directly and not limited through the senses, it has no limits and therefore our joy has not limits. Joy can be and should be thousands of times greater than the greatest joy we have ever experienced in sex.

I would suggest two things: First, to know the foregoing. Second, moderation, or even restraint, if possible, until one constantly has more joy than sex can give. Then it is easy to let go of it because you don't want to be limited in your joy. You want to keep on increasing it until you reach the ultimate joy.

An illiterate person has a much better chance of achieving total freedom because he's not clogged by accrued, accumulated encrustrations of dogma, doctrine, education, ideas. The less ideas we have, the less education we have, the less demand we have to behave in accordance with the world, and therefore we're freer to dive into ourselves.

The less cobwebs we have in the way of seeing ourselves the less we accept from society, because society is very much in the wrong direction. So anything it gives us becomes an obstacle.

The start of the feelings of failure comes from the earliest days. Our parents tell us what to do, they tell us what not to do. Every time we want to do something and they say, "Don't," we feel we can't, we don't know how.

If we don't want to do something and they say, "Do," again we feel that we don't know.

All the "doing" and "don'ting" by parents gives us the feeling that we can't, we don't know, from the first days on. And this continues because it goes on through everyone's life.

Every teacher has it as part of his make-up that we cannot do. So they tell us what to do, and repeat it, and pound it into us, and they continue that negativity that started at infancy.

So maybe ninety-nine per cent of us have a feeling of failure that we can't do. We don't know how.

When we look at ourselves as we really are, and discover what we are, we discover that all things are possible unto us, that all intelligence is available to us, that we have a direct line to omniscience, to omnipotence. And the only thing that keeps us from using it are these preindoctrinated dictums from our parents and teachers: Do. Don't.

So, by discovering ourselves we see how ridiculous it is to hold on to the concept that we cannot. And when we see that everything is possible, methodically those concepts are dropped.

There should be no negative words in any language—no "can'ts," no "don'ts," no "not's." Really it would be a terrific thing if we took them out of the language.

You'll discover that you can say everything you want to say in a positive way. Think only what you want, and that is all that you will get.

All in all, it's the inabilities that are pounded into us from birth on that limit us. Our parents have it; their parents gave it to them. It goes on and on and on, unconsciously being handed down to those whom we think we love so much.

## *LOVE IS A FREEING OF THE OTHER ONE*

I've experienced everything I talk about; that's why it's effective when I talk to others. If I had read it in a book, it would have no import to the one I'm speaking to. But when one experiences it, then tells it, as that one tells it, that infinite power that he has gained is right behind it.

There is a power in his word, even when it is written down after it is said.

But it is felt even more so when it is person to person.

Man is really infinite, and considers himself the opposite. Just quiet your mind enough and discover that which is just behind your mind—your omniscience. Wherever you are, you can use every incident, every relationship to grow by. Just don't stop seeking.

Seeking should be a twenty-four hour quest. Almost everything you're doing is unfree behavior. Examine it and let go of it. Every time you see non-love, turn it to love. Only when you are all-loving are you free.

Get to the place where no one and nothing can disturb you. Take full responsibility for what's happening to you. Get the habit of bringing the unconscious causative thought up into consciousness, so that you can drop it and be free of it.

I developed this. Every time anything unpleasant would happen to me, I would say, "What did I do to cause this?" Immediately the causative thought would come up, I would see it and drop it.

I was driving to Los Angeles with Bill Cass. We had been driving all day and night, and I was tired. We were nearing San Bernardino.

Bill said, "Lester, do your eyes hurt you?" I was tired so I didn't even answer, but I was listening to him.

Then the radio announced high smog in that area. And a second time Bill asked, "Lester, are your eyes smarting?" Again, being very tired, I didn't answer. However, his thought went into me, subconsciously.

The next day my eyes were burning and tearing. As I lay back on the bed with closed eyes in a Los Angeles motel, I asked myself, "Now what did I do to cause this?"

Then I heard Bill saying it the first time. I reversed it.

Then I heard the radio saying it. I reversed that.

And I heard him saying it the second time and again I reversed it. I opened my eyes and there was no more burning, no tearing. And that was the end of it!

You have to reverse everything you hear that's negative, otherwise it goes in subconsciously. You reverse it by dropping the negative and then asserting the positive. "My eyes are fine, my eyes are perfect."

If, when Bill had asked me whether my eyes were smarting, I had answered, "My eyes are fine," everything would've been okay then. I would not have accepted subconsciously that smog causes my eyes to smart and tear.

Always reverse the negatives that you hear, each time as you hear them. We live in a time when there is so much negative emphasis all around us, that it's necessary to do this, if we want a good, happy life.

Because of so much negativity in the world, it's very difficult to get quiet. You really have to isolate. However, you can isolate in New York City.

Isolation from the world is dogged determination to avoid the outer worldly direction and dive deeply into the inner direction of seeking your real Self—so much so, that you keep your direction and attention constantly inward.

One day we'll all wake up to the dream, see that it was a dream, and laugh at the whole thing.

Meanwhile, in the dream I'm trying to wake others out of it, if they want to wake up.

I feel no urgency. But for those who want it, for the rest of me who wants this, now the teaching is available. I would gladly give them my hand and pull them up to awareness if they would go it, if they would take the direction and work at it as a daily routine—continuing to grow by getting freer and freer every day, until they're totally free.

## *LOVE IS ACCEPTANCE*

People who surrender to Jesus get an experience which is delightful, wonderful. It feels right. Associated with it are love and good feelings. These should be expanded.

However, the young people having no complete methodology to do it, cannot continue their growth. If they don't have a complete way, a complete method to follow, they cannot make the goal.

Growth must be continuous until the ultimate is achieved. It must be daily. If you are not going forward, you are necessarily going backward. Sustained growth is absolutely necessary, if you want to achieve the goal. And for this you must know the complete way.

I think this thought might be an aid to those who are so uplifted by Jesus: Don't believe in Jesus, but believe as Jesus believed. Emulate Jesus.

Behave as Jesus did.

Also, the highest point of His way was the Resurrection, the attaining of immortality. The Crucifixion was only a step to the Resurrection.

Seek to attain what He attained—immortality!

Orthodox religions are good in that they teach God and good.

I go farther. I try to teach from the top. I say, God is all and God is perfect. If God is all, that certainly must include us.

Orthodox religions are led by too many people who don't have the realization or revelation of this perfection.

Preaching of sin should never be preached.

A preacher should tell people what great, infinite beings they are, made in the image of God—not that they are lowly sinners. It's terribly destructive to man to tell him he's no good, when, in truth, he's just the opposite! He's infinitely good in his basic nature, and this ought to be brought out.

Since God is all, our basic beingness is God, and goodness and love are our inherent nature.

Yet any religion is ahead of all other studies because it speaks of God and good. Science speaks of the machine as God. Materiality speaks of money and fame as God. Religion is ahead of psychology, philosophy and the like, because it's in a more correct direction.

Beginning with "Genesis," the Bible is the story of our descent as God into gods, and then into man. "Revelation" is just the reverse; it tells of the seven states that man goes through to return to his God-state.

The Bible was originally very good, very high and inspiring, with specific methodology, as it should be. But because it was outlawed and driven underground during the Dark Ages, and also because so many people without full understanding retranslated it, most of the methodology has been left out.

Where is the methodology in the Bible? That's the most important thing: How to do it!

Only in Eastern teaching has the methodology been preserved.

Our Bible is also codified. The Book of "Revelation" is code based on inspirational revelation. Even ministers who have spent their lives studying it cannot understand "Revelation," the most important chapter of the Bible.

I've always advised people to get the Red Letter Edition of The New Testament, and read only the red letters. The Red Letter Edition has everything said by Jesus printed in red—the rest in black. There you have set out the very best of the Bible, the direct words of Jesus.

If Jesus walked down the street today, hardly anyone would recognize Him because of their preconceived, possibly Hollywoodian ideas of what Jesus is. Instead of trumpeting king, He is the most humble individual you could ever meet—quiet, modest and unassuming. However, if you communicated with Him you would definitely notice that he's not usual.

The signs would be inner rather than visible. A receptive individual will feel His power. His magnetism, His love.

Jesus came only to show us the way back to our Godhead. He came to show us the way to our immortality and limitlessness, and He taught those things that would get us there.

He said, "Greater things than these, ye shall do," implying that we will do things even greater than the things He was doing.

He set an example for us to follow. But the example was for us to follow in His footsteps, and to do what He did. And through that be what He is.

If you surrender to Jesus, surrender cannot be lip service. Surrender to Jesus means carrying out His will and His way, which amounts to living as a Christ!

I knew there were men before me who had discovered what I discovered, like Jesus, and they are still around.

They do exist in a body, one made of finer substance than the physical body. They are still with the world, helping those of us who want help. Being in the higher realm, they are far more helpful because they can be anywhere at any moment.

They are conscious of the fact that separateness is a dream. They are conscious of their commitment to help those in the dream wake up out of the dream—and know that they too, are the infinite One.

There is never a time when these great ones are not offering their hands. It's called grace. To the degree that we open ourselves to it, to that degree we receive it.

It's gotten by one way only—through surrender. Not my will, but Thy will be done. It's pushing the ego sense to the background, and letting it go, for the time being. That allows Them in.

You see, the ego sense is a stubborn conviction that the little me knows. When we get that out of the way, then help comes in.

The thing that allows us to surrender is the desire to surrender. It's simple. When we really desire to surrender, we do it. But the desire to be this big-shot ego-body is so strong with us, that we don't easily let go of it. It is usually stronger than the desire to meet with the great ones.

If you can surrender, you can meet with Jesus.

Every meeting you have with these great ones leaves you other than what you were before. They always do something for you. They leave you with a tremendous new revelation.

They never leave you the same. And this is the way you can tell whether the meeting is real, or whether it's just your imagination.

It's difficult, to tell a true teacher from others because he usually is humble and his qualities are inner qualities. Of the things to look for, I would say the greatest is a teacher's inner, imperturbable peace. He does not go up on praise, nor down on condemnation.

Next, he sees everything with equalmindedness. Everyone is treated alike and the same by him. He shows not one ounce of favoritism towards anyone, whether that one is an angel, a villain, or an animal.

Contentedness and complete acceptance of all that is, are also signs to look for. Lastly, he gives his knowledge—freely.

The path is the way to the ultimate truth of man.

A Master is one who has become a master over his body and a master over his mind, and thus has achieved the ultimate freedom.

The word "guru" means teacher. With a capitalized "G" (G-U-R-U) Gee you are you—it means a fully realized teacher, or a Master.

A Master can help us go free.

Could you imagine the ocean to be infinity? Well, we, the ocean of beingness, imagine little tiny circles around parts of us that we call drops; and this drop says, "I am separate from that drop and separate from all the other drops." It's an imagined circle around part of the ocean calling itself a drop.

But actually, every drop is the ocean. It has all the qualities of the ocean: It's wet, it's salty, it's $H_2O$, and so forth. And everything that the infinity is, we are.

You see, it's a false apparency that the drops are separate from the ocean.

When you see the truth, only then do you understand this.

All the masters never lose sight of the oneness or allness. But they choose to play-act a game of separateness, to help the rest of their Self that's asleep to wake up out of the dream of separateness.

It's that simple. Point of view changes when you get realization—from separateness to oneness. Simple! Simple! Simple!

Before everything, is separate from you. After, everything is in you. Before, the world seems intensely real. After, you'll see the panorama of life as a dream. You'll know it's dream texture and you'll let the dream run.

Then, when you're ready to leave the dream, you gather in all your forces, and with a big smile on your face, you consciously exit the body into your immortality.

The real you is your very own real Self, the "I" of you as you really are. It is not confined to the body or mind that you now think you are.

Our real beingness, our real Self, is like the screen in a cinema show. Your real Self is the changeless screen and the flitting pictures are the world.

The Self of us the screen, never moves but all the pictures on the screen do.

When you're looking at the characters on the screen and all the play that goes on, the fires, floods, and bombs don't touch the screen. The fires don't burn it; the floods don't wet it; the bombs don't destroy it.

That screen, like our very own Self, is changeless and untouchable, perfect.

But superimposed on the Self, as there is superimposed on this screen, is all this action. When you wake up to the fact that this cinema show of our universe is only as solid as a picture show, from that point on, you know world action to be as real as the movies.

My wish for everyone is that everyone attain the highest state possible, so that here on earth we have that heaven that everyone dreams of, where life is beautiful, life is easy and everyone has the greatest love and respect for each other!

This would cause all misery to drop away, all sickness to disappear, all thoughts of war and destructiveness to be eliminated from our minds, and in place of it, just the opposite: love, beauty and joy.

To sum up, my overall wish is for everyone (the rest of me!) to fully know what I know so that all misery and unhappiness is at an end.

Love,

Lester

Written in 1972

## *HERE'S HOW PEOPLE USE THE RELEASE TECHNIQUE TO HAVE MORE ABUNDANCE WITH EASE*

"The most pronounced, tangible evidence that I'm getting, only through using the method, is in the monetary aspects of my business. I'm on a commission basis only, and I've earned as much in the first quarter of this year as I did in all of last year."

*Karen Brock, Woodland Hills, CA*
*President, Brock Enterprises*

"I took The Release Technique because I was under a lot of business and personal pressure. I find now that I'm more relaxed, easier in all my relationships and making a lot more money with much less effort—playing smarter, not harder."

*Tom Beyers, Scottsdale, AZ*
*Senior Vice President, First Federal Mortgage Company*

"My business has tripled since learning the Abundance Course, yet I'm spending most of my time traveling and having fun all the time. The Technique is so powerful, I've had my entire family learn the Technique. I also got rid of 20 years of asthma. Last month I made over 1 million dollars using this Technique."

*Jim Whitman, World Traveler*

"I have regained my focus on abundance thanks to The Abundance Course. Customers are calling me to advertise on my radio show—big time! I recommend it to all who want abundance, riches, success, happiness and health. It really does work."

*Jacquie Solomon, Phoenix, AZ*
*Radio Hostess, KFNX*

"I'm excited!" I have already made over $7,000 and I am working on a deal now I expect to triple that...Anyone can do it. All that the Abundance course claims is true and then some. I can't imagine everyone not taking this course."

*Kathy Shoden, Los Angeles, CA*
*Sales and Marketing*

"I just completed the Abundance Course for the first time last weekend. On the second day, I received an offer for a house I have been trying to sell for three years. Before the course ended, I received three offers on the house. My sales results have been amazing—I've had the biggest month I ever had, and that's just in one week! I can't imagine anyone not wanting to learn The Easy Way."

*Gayle Henderson, Scottsdale, AZ*
*Russ Lyon Realty Co.*

# "VAST ABUNDANCE IS WITHIN YOU... WHY NOT JOIN IN ON THE FUN?

## HAVE ABUNDANT HEALTH

"I took the Abundance Course to have more financial abundance in my life. No only did I get that big time, but I had chronic pain in my jaw for 6 years. I was able to get rid of it the very first evening of practicing The Technique. My golf improved, I lowered my score by 14 points in two weeks. This course is worth millions—Don't wait. Call them right now!"

*Roger Brunnetti, Woodland Hills, CA*
*Marketing Consultant*

I have had a full recovery from a boating accident since taking the course. I did not have full range-of-motion in my left arm, I do now and I have been able to stop taking 14 different pills."

*Raul Marmol, Claremont, CA*

"During the second day, I worked on an injured foot that had been bothering me for years. I was wearing a bandage and a sandal. The next day I was able to wear shoes and it didn't hurt me at all! I'm not angry at anyone, and I like myself more, and I feel joy all the time. Wow!"

*Cathryn Willmeng, Phoenix, AZ*
*Real Estate Appraiser*

"I let go of a lower back pain I had been suffering with for a long time during the third day of the course. I even took off my back support—WOW, what a course."

*Gary Sylvester, San Diego, CA*
*Telecommunications*

## BE IN TOTAL CONTROL OF YOUR LIFE

"On Sunday morning (during the course), I woke up with the knowledge that I had found the tools that empower me to take back control of my life, and that's not a goal—that's a fact."

*Linda Carella, Los Angeles, CA*
*V.P. Marketing, Tova Corp.*

"Acceptance expanded, trust expanded, love expanded, freedom is and continuously unfolds easily! I also received five checks in the mail yesterday—and money and joy just keep rolling in. I also have a major art show this week at the Scottsdale Art Center and it just happened with ease."

*Monica Martinez, Phoenix, AZ*
*artist*

"This course helped me bring back the value of more consistent releasing. It has given me the awareness to use the tools I have for releasing with ease. Thank you for putting such a practical spin on the method. My life is so much richer for having use of the tools and Lester's wisdom."

*Rosalie Lurie, Los Angeles, CA, Fundraiser*

"I no longer judge myself and others. I no longer feel guilty about anything; I love myself and others. I'm experiencing peace and joy more and more. I can't imagine anyone not taking this fabulous course."

*Scott Jones, Mission Viejo, CA*
*Advertising Executive*

"I gained the ability to stop being counterproductive in my life. I can now erase any attitude of 'I never win.' It enabled me to take control of myself–wow!"

*Kathy Mullen, El Segundo, CA*

## *RID YOURSELF OF FAILURE HABITS*

"I actually let go of beating myself up—I hadn't thought it was possible. I feel exhilarated and energetic after years of fatigue. I have more clarity and peace and improved self confidence—I have a feeling of 'I can' after years of depressions and anxiety—Thank you Lester and Larry."

*Luz Ugalde Fortner, Ventura, CA*

"I've taken many lessons, but it wasn't until I took The Release Technique that I really, really got on track. Wow–I really didn't know what I was missing! Releasing is the greatest, and our natural way...Don't miss this opportunity."

*Ron Hamady, Los Angeles, CA, Movie Producer*

## *RID YOURSELF OF FEAR AND GAIN CLARITY*

I unlocked my fear, lack and scarcity feelings that stopped me from having abundance for years. It was powerful and fun and easy. I can't imagine anyone not taking this course—it's a must."

*Joseph Harrington, Los Angeles, Ca*
*Psychologist*

"My clarity in life improved dramatically. I see where I am and where to go next. My abundance improved just in that one weekend—I wish all could attend."

*Craig Davis, Winnetka, CA, School Psychologist*

"I had severe anxiety when I would get on the freeway. It was preventing me from having a life. Then I took The Abundance Course. On the first day, I dumped the phobia. It was so simple that it was almost hard to believe it could be so easy! I now look at life in such a way that it becomes magical. I recommend it to all."

*Lauren Brent, Los Angeles, CA*
*Esthetician*

"I was able to retire from a job I had for years, and I feel terrific about it! I'm using the 'Butt' system and it works. Thank you, the course is the greatest."

*Charles Jones, Washington, DC*
*Psychotherapist*

"I released about worrying about the future. My life really works!"

*Bebe Young, Paramount, CA*
*Businesswoman*

"I just completed The Abundance Course. My understanding gets clearer and clearer. My decision process is fantastic, and I'm having fun all the time. My business has tripled, and I have more time to do what I want. It's easy—anyone can do it."

*Judy Smith Whitman, Scottsdale, AZ*
*Art Dealer*

## FEEL LOVE ANYTIME YOU WANT

"These past few weeks have been especially wonderful—'Joyous' is the true word. More and more I do see myself as one with everything. Right now, Larry, I feel as if I'm going to explode with joy—and I can't stop laughing! All is well! All should join in on the fun."

*Clara Sida-McCoy, Glendale, AZ*
*Housewife/Secretary*

"The new work that is being done on abundance is fantastic. I'm just busting with happiness and doing and having what I want all the time."

*Cecilia Gallagher, Scottsdale, AZ*
*Business Developer*

"I never thought I could feel this good about myself. I now have a tool I can use each day of my life."

*Yvonne Medina, Los Angeles, CA*
*Client Service Genetics Institute*

## UNLOCK WHAT'S HOLDING YOU BACK FROM HAVING TOTAL ABUNDANCE AND JOY IN YOUR LIFE—ONCE AND FOR ALL LEARN TO TRUST YOURSELF

"By the end of Day 2, I achieved a sense of deep calm. While driving home, I found I wasn't so irritated by other drivers and I remained unperturbed. My boyfriend commented on the youthful, lighter look on my face over dinner."

*Kim LaChance, Lawndale, CA*
*Therapist*

"I have been going through books and seminars for so long. This course allowed me to see that life can be without problems. The future is wonderful now."

*Pirayeh Shaban, Pasadena, CA*
*Coordinator*

## *IMPROVE RELATIONSHIPS*

"I am able to release my anger at my girlfriend whenever she gets angry/jealous about our relationship. Our relationship has greatly improved in a short time."

*Jay Torres, Culver City, CA*
*Salesman*

"My relationship with my children has greatly improved. I am able to handle disgruntled clients without being uptight. I lost my craving for smoking and stopped smoking in the first day of the course."

*Thomas Mitchel, Los Angeles, CA*
*Investment Advisor*

"Everything is working for me with ease—my relationships are getting better, my business is exploding with ease, abundance just is and it's easy!"

*Shawna Leach-Lugo, Phoenix, AZ*
*Artist*

"I can allow myself to love people for who they are, no matter what."

*John Cullen, Lake-in-the-Hills, IL*
*Contractor*

## *MORE REPORTS FROM THE ABUNDANCE COURSE GRADUATES*
## *DROP UNWANTED HABITS*

"A few weeks after learning The Release Technique, I completely stopped my chain smoking habit and the craving hasn't come back in 15 years since stopping."

*Don Janklow, Westlake Village, CA*
*President, Janklow & Associates*

"I have learned to relax by releasing, and an unexpected gain has been that I no longer have a desire for alcohol—it feels good."

*Jack Dimalante, New York*

"I lost five pounds during the first week of the course without thinking about it!"

*Lloyd Scott, Dallas, TX*

"I used this method when I was feeling hunger, and I no longer feel the desire to eat."

*Rita Recken, Glandorf, OH*

## *ELIMINATE STRESS*

"Sleeping better than I have in years. I quit taking drugs for my arthritis and feel better without them."

*Raymond Hanson, Los Angeles, CA*

"I connected with the ease of releasing. I simply didn't know how much resistance I had. By Sunday, I had so much energy it was great and after only four hours of sleep. I feel lighter and happier."

*Ariana Attie, Los Angeles, CA*
*Legal Secretary*

"The first weekend I discovered my feeling of fatigue could be alleviated, and I drove 200 miles without the sleepiness and feeling of heaviness that so often plagued me."

*Ruth A. Riegel, Chicago, IL*

"I had several physical ailments including migraine headaches, diverticulitis, gout and severe hypoglycemia, and the week after taking the course was scheduled for surgery. But within a few days after beginning to release, the surgical condition disappeared and never re-appeared. My other physical problems cleared up. I believe these good effects are due to the stress reduction brought about by using the Method."

*Dr. David Hawkins, Manhasset, NY*
*Medical Director, The North Nassau Mental Health Center*

I think it is becoming evident, in my observation, that the techniques learned in the program were beneficial to people who work under the stress and strain that we do in the Investment Banking Industry. I have personally benefited, especially when I ran the New York City Marathon shortly after an illness.

*Thomas J. Kitrick*
*Vice President Training and Development*
*Goldman, Sachs & Co.*